WINNING RUGBY

Effective Drills for Improving Player Skills

Brian Quistberg

NTC/Contemporary Publishing Group

Library of Congress Cataloging-in-Publication Data

Quistberg, Brian
Winning rugby : effective drills for improving player skills / Brian Quistberg.
p. cm.
ISBN 1-57028-181-5
1. Rugby football—Training. 2. Rugby football—Coaching. I. Title.
GV945.8.Q85 1998
796.333'2—dc21 98-3016
CIP

To my wife, Randee, my best friend,
and to my children, Jenelle, Kirsten, and Jaime,
for their love and support

Cover design by Nick Panos

Interior design by Chad Woolums

Published by Masters Press
A division of NTC/Contemporary Publishing Group, Inc.
4255 West Touhy Avenue, Lincolnwood (Chicago), Illinois 60646-1975 U.S.A.

Printed in the United States of America
International Standard Book Number: 1-57028-181-5
99 00 01 02 03 04 CU 19 18 17 16 15 14 13 12 11 10 9 8 7 6 5 4 3 2 1

CONTENTS

DRILLS

FOREWORD

Brian Quistberg maintains a unique involvement with the game of rugby. Experienced as a player, coach, administrator, and promoter of the sport, he combines a high level of technical expertise with a practical knowledge of how to make the game itself more enjoyable to play.

The result comes to life in *Winning Rugby*—a tremendous resource for anyone interested in the game of rugby, regardless of their level of experience. Brian places his emphasis on presenting activities that allow the reader to develop an individual understanding of the sport, activities that are readily applicable for team use on the field of play or in the classroom. Simply put, his ideas are not just easy to follow but easily adapted to a variety of settings, general or specific.

The extensive work that has gone into compiling the information contained in this book is a reflection of Brian Quistberg's enthusiasm for rugby. If there is one resource you can look to for a simple, practical, and effective guide to understanding and teaching rugby, this is it.

Mark Harper
Former Head Coach – University of Waterloo; Lifetime Member of UWRFC; Coach of OUAA Champions and OUAA Coach of the Year (1985); Provincial Regional Coach/ Selector; Six-time Coach of WCSSAA Rugby Champions; Co-convenor WCSSAA League; Coach of Oxford University "Cuppers" Champions (Ontario, Canada)

ACKNOWLEDGMENTS

I'd like to take this opportunity to thank those who made this book possible:

To begin with, I'd like to express thanks to my family—a loving appreciation to my wife, Randee, for her support and devotion throughout my career as a player and coach, and special thanks to my children, Jenelle, Kirsten, and Jamie, for allowing me the time to sit down and complete this project.

To Mark Harper, who has been an inspiration and a team player in all our rugby endeavors together over the years (remember Edinburgh) as well as a true friend who shares a love for the game that rivals my own. Much of this book is credited to Mark, the result of his assistance in collecting effective drills and his invaluable contribution to the local rugby community by helping me to share this information. It is worth noting that Mark was the person who first approached me to come out and coach the University of Waterloo many years ago. I have since learned a great deal from him and continue to do so. The years of involvement at the University of Waterloo bring back fond memories, and I'm confident that the future holds many more.

To "Coop," whose helpful suggestions played a vital role in developing the manuscript; to all the many coaches and players I've had the opportunity to play for and with; to Oakville Trafalgar High School, where rugby grew to become the most successful and most popular sport, largely due to Coach Gary Turnbull, God's gift to rugby, a coach who inspired a great many athletes, myself included, many of these athletes having gone on to represent Canada and many more continuing their involvement with the game to this day.

And finally to these individual coaches and friends whom I'd like to take the time to recognize: Coach Bob "Fly" Nye (for making the game so much fun); Coach Neil McCartney (for guiding my university playing career); Coach Derek Humphrey (for teaching me so much); Tom and Tim McCleary (for being such great friends and upstanding members of the Brantford Old Boys Rugby Club); the Waterloo Rugby Football Club and all the local coaches and young athletes in Waterloo County (for astounding support promoting the growth of the game); the many friends and fellow rugby players at McMaster and Queen's University (for all the good times).

INTRODUCTION: RUGBY AT A GLANCE

THE NEED FOR A RUGBY DRILL BOOK

The Rugby Union has experienced major worldwide growth in recent years, especially in North America. The basic appeal of the game itself is partly responsible for the rise in interest. Statistics show significant increases in the number of players at all levels and backgrounds: this includes high school and university teams, clubs, and specifically the number of female teams that have recently developed. There are many specific characteristics of the sport which I feel have led to this resurgence.

To begin with, the basic rules of play are quite simple. There are no expensive equipment requirements and the field of play can be catered to whatever space is available. The combination of athletic attributes that rugby demands also seems to attract many players—skills such as speed, stamina, contact, and intelligence. This is not to mention that rugby is unique in that it allows for athletes of varying shapes and sizes to discover an effective role on the field of play.

Laymen generally have a number of misconceptions about the game. Many assume that rugby is a brutally violent and dangerous sport. However, if you take a closer look as I have done, you, like thousands of others in North America and worldwide, will discover quite the contrary. Rugby is a sport that gives a player the opportunity for lifetime involvement. Just check out the number of over-35, over-40, and even over-50 teams out there. If the budding athlete can get past initial assumptions, he or she is in for quite a pleasant surprise.

Despite all of these developments, there are few resources available on the market for coaches to consult when it comes to rugby. This is an unfortunate situation—after all, it is important that a coach have a variety of drills and lead-up activities at his disposal in order to challenge players, keep them motivated, improve their understanding of the game, and promote and maintain an enjoyable atmosphere in practice situations. For these reasons I decided to compile an informative drill book in hopes of providing a resource to fill this void, to provide coaches with a quick and easy source of reference for enhancing the training skills of those players participating in the sport of rugby.

So who exactly is this book intended for—the beginner, the intermediate, or the advanced player/team? The answer to that question is simple—it is designed for all of the above.

Because any coach at any level can benefit from adding to their repertoire of practice drills, *Winning Rugby* promises to assist coaches at all levels—high school, club, university, and college ranks alike. Not only that, this is a book that will prove useful for teachers of physical education as well as sport instructors interested in teaching rugby in the school setting at any level.

You are sure to find that each and every drill addressed throughout this book is designed to satisfy a specific objective. You will also discover that all the relative information is presented clearly and completely so as to provide effective guidelines for teaching and improving a variety of team and individual skills.

GAME BASICS

OBJECTIVE

The object of the game is to advance the ball down the field by running it forward, kicking it ahead, or passing it sideways/backward to a teammate, who may then run the ball forward in the attempt to score points. At the same time, a team seeks to stop the opposition from achieving the same result.

SCORING

To gain points, players must score in the following ways:

- **Score a try (5 points)** — carry the ball over the goal line and touch the ball to the ground in the opposition in-goal area (end zone).
- **Score a conversion (2 points)** — following a try, kick the ball directly through the opposition goalpost uprights by means of a placekick or dropkick; the kick must be taken out directly from where the try was scored.
- **Score a penalty kick (3 points)** — following a penalty, kick the ball directly through the opposition goalpost uprights.
- **Score a drop goal (3 points)** — kick the ball directly through the opposition goalpost uprights at any time during play; the kick must be preceded by the player bouncing the ball off the ground.

BASIC RULES

The basic rules that all players must abide by are as follows:

- A player must always be beside or behind the ball; otherwise he is "offside" and not allowed to be involved with the play.
- A player stops the opposition by tackling them or taking the ball outside the playing area (this is accomplished by kicking the ball or pushing a player in possession of the ball out-of-bounds).
- No dangerous play is permitted (no jumping on other players, no kicking at other players, no tackles that are too high).
- Once a player has been tackled, he must release the ball and cannot play it until he has regained his feet.

NUMBER OF PLAYERS/GAME LENGTH

A rugby match may vary in terms of players on the field and game length as such:

- **15's** — there are 15 players per team (8 forwards, 7 backs); the game consists of two 40-minute halves.
- **7's** — there are 7 players per team (3 forwards, 4 backs); the game consists of two 7-minute halves.

THE FIELD

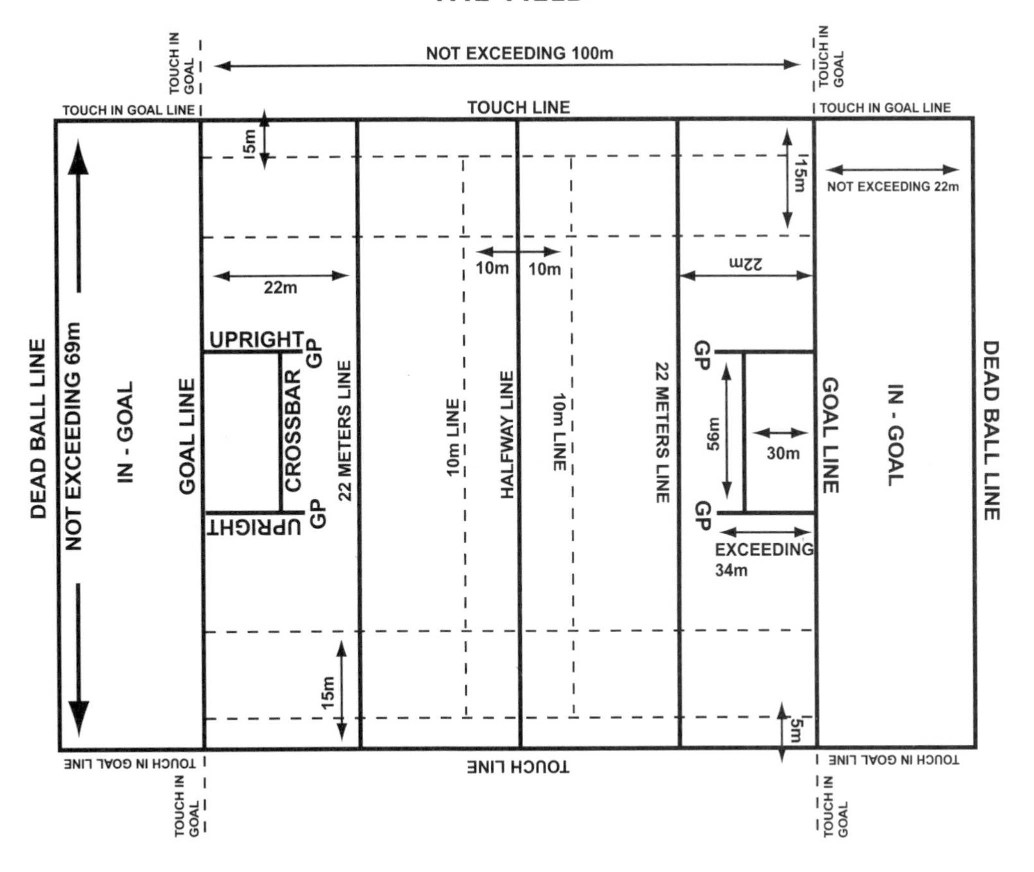

STARTING PLAY

The basic elements of play are as follows:

- **Kickoff** — play begins with a kickoff from center (the ball must travel at least 10 meters).
- **Scrum** — after a minor infraction, forwards from both teams bind together in a tight formation. The team that has not committed the infraction puts the ball into the scrum. Both teams then attempt to hook the ball back to their side as well as push the opposition back.
- **Lineout** — when the ball goes out-of-bounds over the sidelines, forwards from both teams line up beside each other and jump, attempting to tip or catch the ball and win possession for their team. The team that does not have possession of the ball when it went out-of-bounds gets to put the ball into play.
- **Penalty kick** — after a major infraction, the non-offending team is given possession of the ball. The opposition must be at least 10 meters back. The non-offending team may then kick the ball downfield, kick for posts, run, pass, or tap the ball and pick it up.

SPECIAL SITUATIONS

The following special situations represent advanced elements of the basic game of rugby. Keep in mind, however, that these situations still remain part of the game at all skill levels.

Ruck

Ruck is the term given to a situation when:

- the ball is on the ground
- one or more players from each team are on their feet and in physical contact, closing around the ball between them

General Rules About Rucks

A player may not:

- handle the ball in a ruck
- jump on others, fall, or collapse a ruck
- interfere with the ball emerging from the ruck if in a prone position on the ground
- join a ruck from his opponents' side or in front of the ball (players must bind when joining a ruck)
- stand beside the ruck in front of the hindmost foot of his own players in the ruck

Purpose of Rules About Ruck

The purpose of the ruck is to provide some guidelines for getting the ball back into play in a congested situation.

Maul

Maul is the term given to a situation when:

- the ball is in a player's hands
- one or more players from each team are positioned on their feet and in physical contact, closing around the players with the ball

General Rules About Mauls

Players may not:

- jump on, fall on, or collapse a maul
- be offside at the maul (same as a ruck)

Purpose of Rules About Maul

The purpose of the maul is to provide some guidelines for getting the ball back into play in a tackle situation.

Scrum

Scrum is the term given to a situation when players from both teams bind together to restart play after a minor infraction has occurred (i.e., the ball is dropped, passed, or knocked forward).

General Rules About Scrums

Scrums require:

- five players must be present (three players in the front row)
- hips must be below shoulders
- players must bind together
- the ball must be put straight into the tunnel

Lineout

Lineout is the term given to the situation when the ball passes out of the sidelines and reenters into play. The team not in possession of the ball when it passed out-of-bounds gets to throw the ball into the lineout.

General Rules About Lineouts

Lineouts require:

- the lineout is formed by at least two players from each team lining up in single lines parallel to each other and directly out from the sidelines
- the team throwing in the ball shall determine the maximum number of players from either team who will line up (no more than seven players)
- there must be half a meter between players from opposite teams
- the lineout stretches out 5 to 15 meters from the sideline
- all players not directly involved in the lineout must be at least 10 meters back from the lineout until it is over
- the ball must be thrown straight between the opposing lines

Penalty

Penalty is the term given to a situation when a major infraction has occurred (i.e., illegal tackle, offside, etc.).

General Rules About Penalties

- the non-offending team puts the ball into play by kicking it any distance from the ground at the location where the penalty occurred
- the non-offending team may kick the ball through the opposition goalpost uprights, kick it out-of-bounds or downfield, or kick it lightly then run
- the offending team must be 10 meters back from the location where the offense occurred and cannot move forward until the ball is moved from the mark at which the offense occurred

TEACHING POINTS

Here are some points to consider when teaching or learning the game of rugby.

Ruck (ball on the ground, the two teams have formed around it)

- enter the ruck in control
- keep head up and hips low
- drive beyond your team's ball, drive the opposition off the ball
- bind onto other players where possible

Maul (ball held in upright tackle, both teams attempt to win possession)

- from the initial contact the ball will be presented
- the first player to arrive must secure the possession by ripping the ball
- the arriving players then support by binding on either side of the maul
- make sure all players bind tightly

Scrummage

- down as eight
- feet positioned before engagement
- firm foundation, hips below shoulders
- bind tightly

Pushing Position (rucks, mauls, or scrummages)

- head up, back straight
- hips below your shoulders to form a wide base
- grasp a fellow teammate or an opposing player with a full bind

Contact

- wide base, stay on feet
- contact and recoil
- move forward, protect the ball, and make it available for support

Passing/Receiving

- reach for the ball and take it early
- stay over the ball
- catch and move ball with fingertips; pass by pushing it using fingertips

Passing Basics

- hands up, pass ball sideways or backward
- catch and pass with fingertips
- transfer ball smoothly and rapidly
- pass ball to space and allow teammate to run onto it

Scrum Half Passes

- keep inside foot near the ball
- maintain a wide base
- grab and extend; don't take extra steps or swing
- vary the speed and length of the pass

Dive Pass

- generally used when it is wet or when the ball is being chased by close-following forwards
- the player picks the ball up and dives in the direction of the pass
- the arms swing in the direction of the receiving player

Tackling

- drive in with shoulder
- head up, to the side, or behind
- wrap with arms and squeeze
- drive legs, taking man to the ground

Sidestep

- executed close to the defender, a sudden change of direction
- consists of: a short step, a hard step-stopping movement in one direction, and a quick, accelerating step away in opposite direction
- generally is a movement to the outside followed by a quick cut back to the inside where the man is beat

Swerve

- executed farther away from the defender (approximately 6 meters or more)
- beat defender to the outside by running on a line to the inside (inside foot crosses outside)

COACHING POINTS

- Keep it simple for the players—use simplified teaching points for teaching the various playing skills.
- Coach all skills to all players.
- Follow the basics—go forward with support.
- Make practice fun regardless of the level of play.
- Be positive with all athletes and fellow coaches.
- Make fitness a key aspect of your training and practice program (this will bring your team greater success and limit injuries).
- Physical practice length should not exceed 1.5 hours.

STEPS FOR USING *WINNING RUGBY*

- Be creative—add, delete, or change suggested drills or lead-up activities.
- Adjust the size of the boundaries for the various drills to meet your specific needs.
- Don't hesitate to try a new drill.
- Try perhaps to add one new drill per training session.
- Try to motivate your players to keep the work rate high during the drills—this will increase the players' fitness level.
- Be sure to point out the positive things your players are doing, then move on to explore new suggestions.
- Remember that there is no substitute for playing the game.

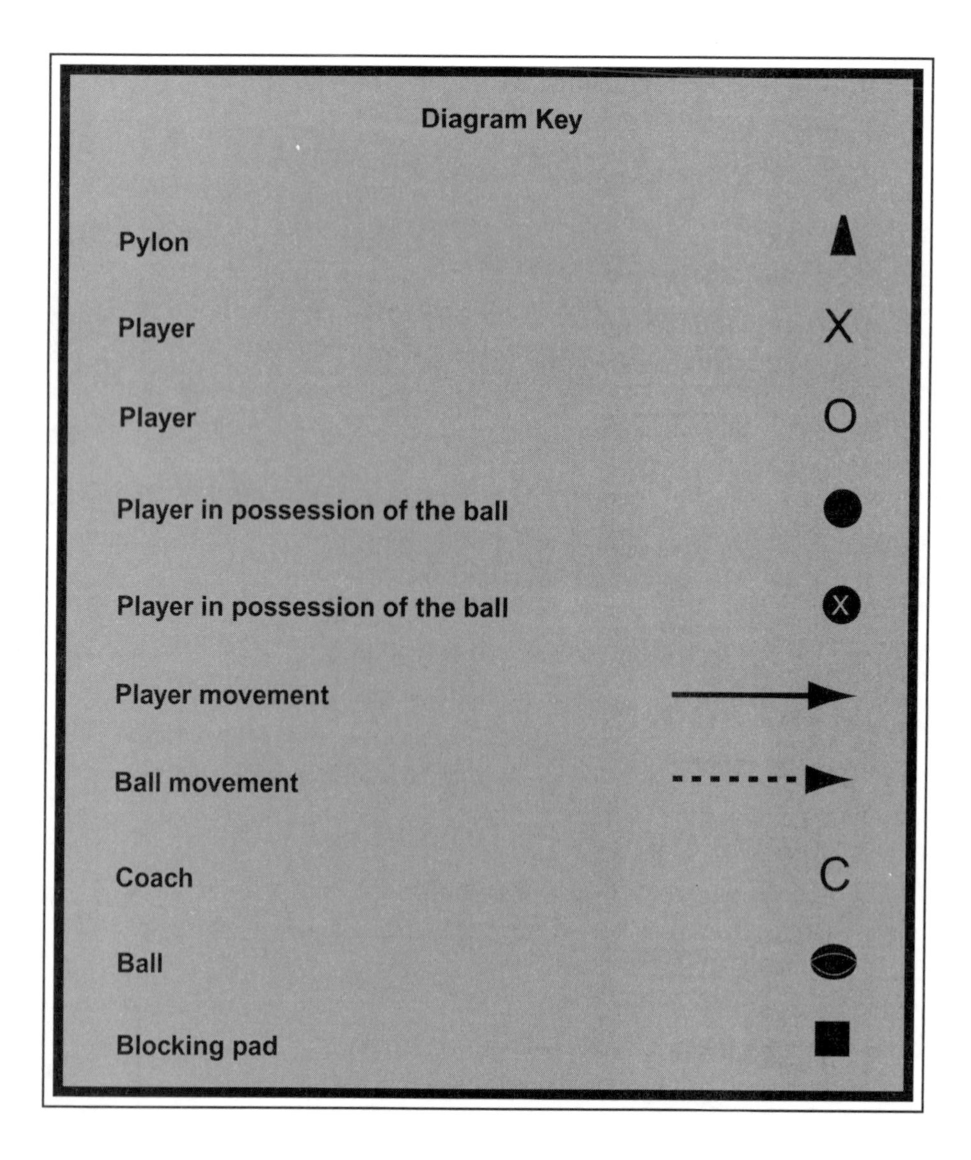

1

HANDLING GAMES

BALL UP AND BACK OUT

OBJECTIVE: Improving ballhandling skills
NUMBER OF PLAYERS: 8 per group
AREA/FIELD: 15 yards × 15 yards
TIME: 5 minutes
EQUIPMENT: 1 ball (per group)

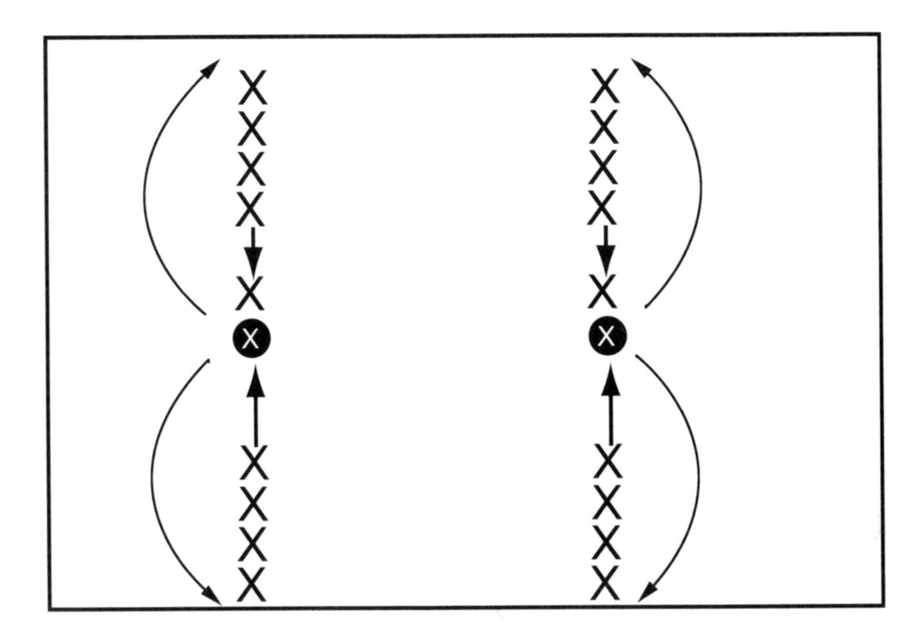

INSTRUCTIONS:

- Organize each group of players in two lines; players should be directly opposite and facing one another.
- Using a single ball for each group, players meet in the center of the line; the player with the ball pops it up to allow the other player to catch it.
- The ball remains in the center as each player quickly catches and pops the ball up for the next player.
- Players must quickly backpedal out of the line (always to the right or the left).

COACHING POINTS:

- Drill may be used as an effective warm-up drill.

2 WANDERING BALL

OBJECTIVE: Improving passing skills
NUMBER OF PLAYERS: 12–16
AREA/FIELD: 20 yards × 20 yards
TIME: 8–10 minutes
EQUIPMENT: 1 ball

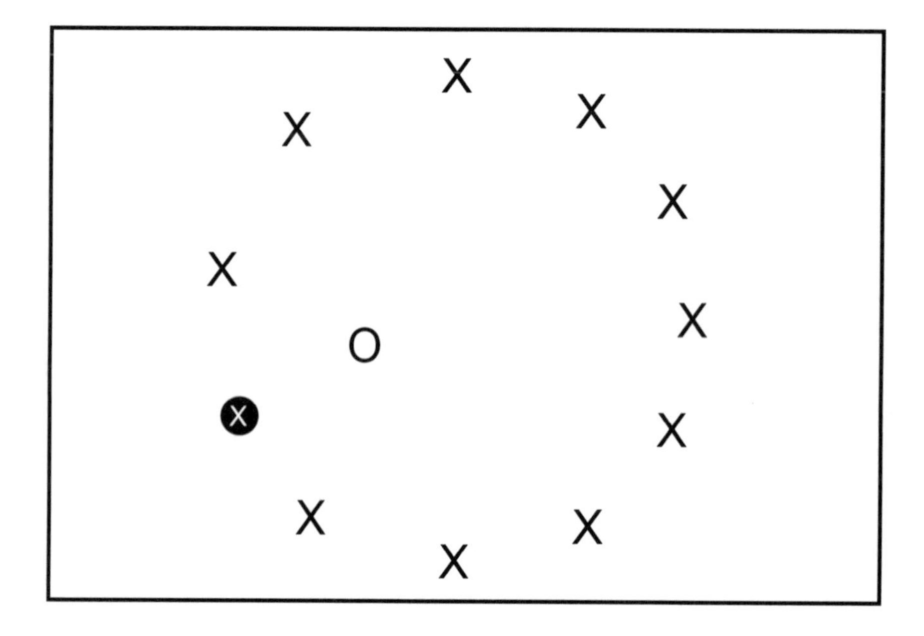

INSTRUCTIONS:

- Organize players in a circle formation with an interceptor on the inside.
- Players attempt to move the ball around the circle without: dropping the ball, allowing an interception, or getting tagged when in possession of the ball.
- Players cannot pass the ball to players immediately on either side.
- The player who makes a bad pass or is tagged then takes the place of the interceptor.

3 KEEP THE BALL MOVING

OBJECTIVE: Improving passing skills

NUMBER OF PLAYERS: 8–12

AREA/FIELD: 20 yards × 20 yards

TIME: 7 minutes

EQUIPMENT: 1 ball (per group)

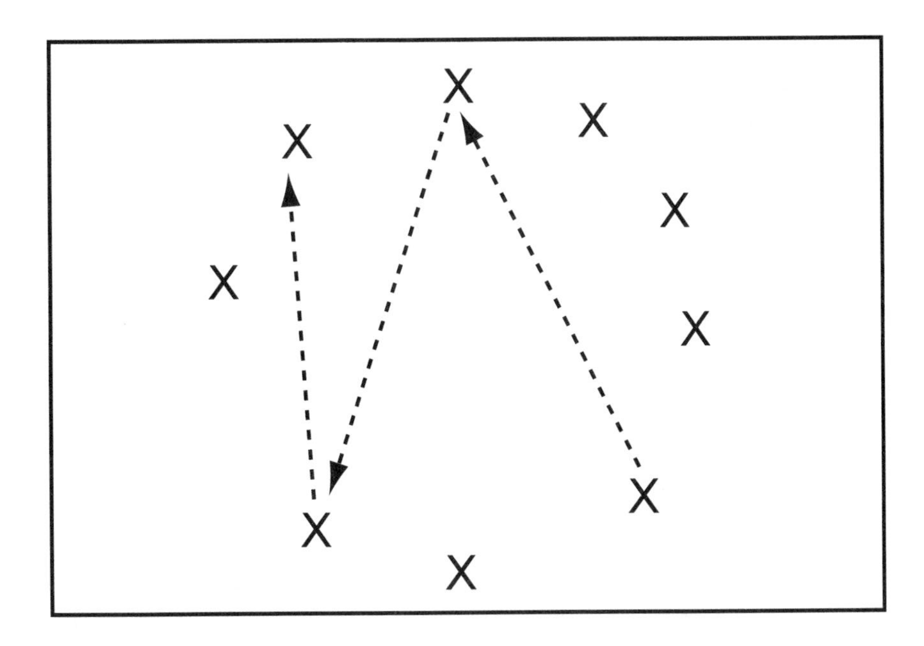

INSTRUCTIONS:

- Organize players in a circle formation.
- Using one ball, a pattern of passing the ball among teammates is set.
- Players attempt to pass the ball as quickly as possible following this pattern.

VARIATIONS:

- Additional balls may be added to the circle.
- Players may move and follow their pass; in this way, each player begins each new circuit at a different location.

4 BALL RACE

OBJECTIVE: Improving passing skills

NUMBER OF PLAYERS: 8 or more

AREA/FIELD: Half field (up to full field)

TIME: 3–4 minutes

EQUIPMENT: 1 ball (per group)

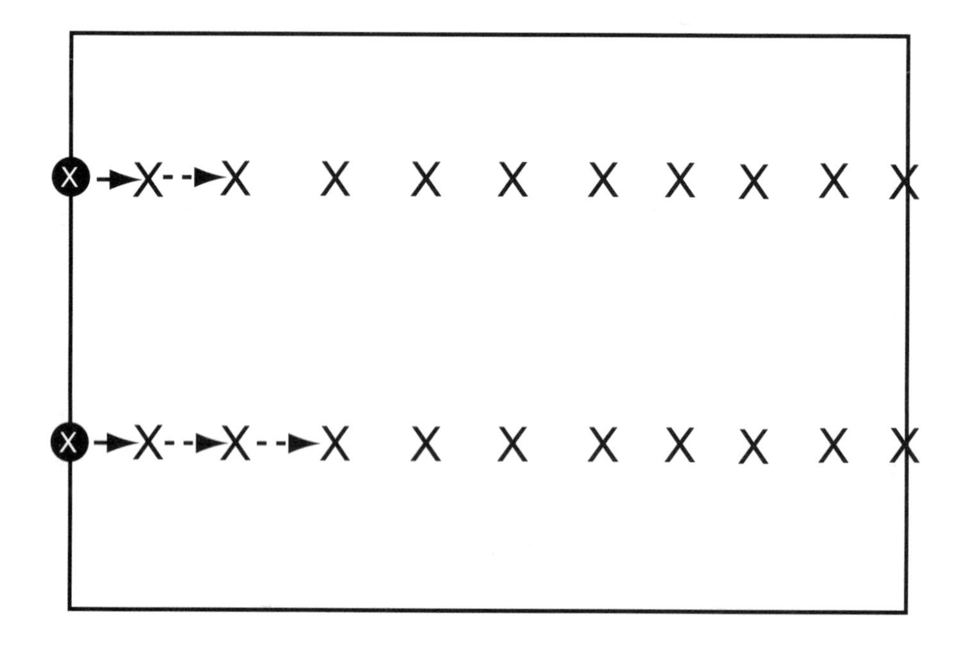

INSTRUCTIONS:

- Organize two teams in single-file lines; players should be across from one another and spread from sideline to sideline (or appropriate distance).
- Each player occupies a static position spaced identical to a player in the opposing team's line.
- Each team races to pass the ball quickly from one end of the line, then back, in an attempt to reach the starting point ahead of the opposition.

COACHING POINTS:

- Drill offers a fun challenge for players (i.e., backs vs. forwards).

5 HOW MANY PASSES

OBJECTIVE: Improving passing skills
NUMBER OF PLAYERS: 8
AREA/FIELD: 4 yards × 4 yards
TIME: 7 minutes
EQUIPMENT: 1 ball (per group), 6 pylons

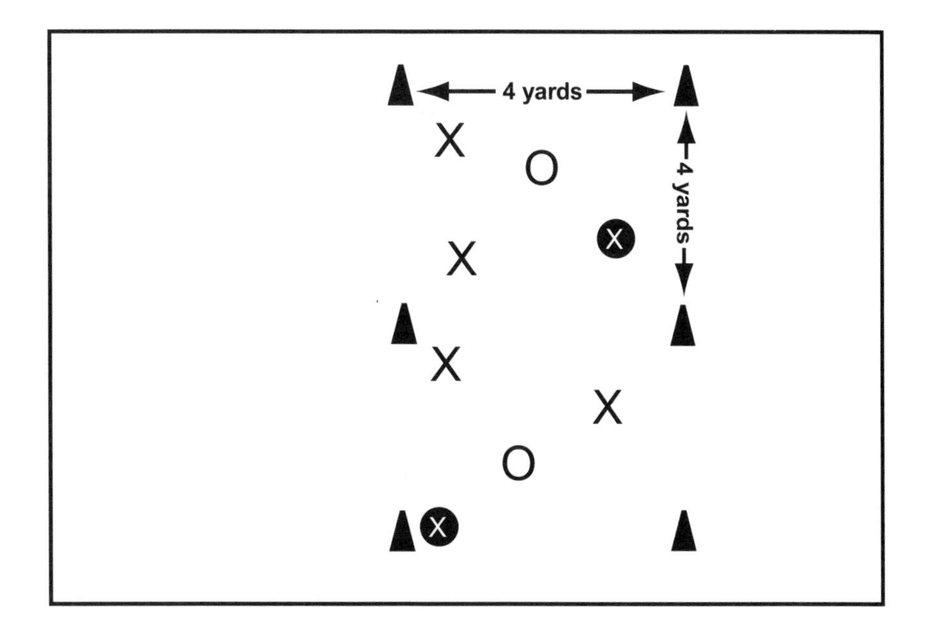

INSTRUCTIONS:

- Organize players in a small grid area.
- Players attempt to pass the ball back and forth while an interceptor tries to pressure the other players into making a poor pass and/or dropping the ball.
- If the ball is intercepted or dropped, the interceptor becomes a passer and the player who made the poor pass becomes the new interceptor.

6 ALL IN PASSING

OBJECTIVE: Improving passing skills
NUMBER OF PLAYERS: 6–12
AREA/FIELD: 6 yards × 6 yards
TIME: 7–10 minutes
EQUIPMENT: 1 ball (per pair), 4 pylons

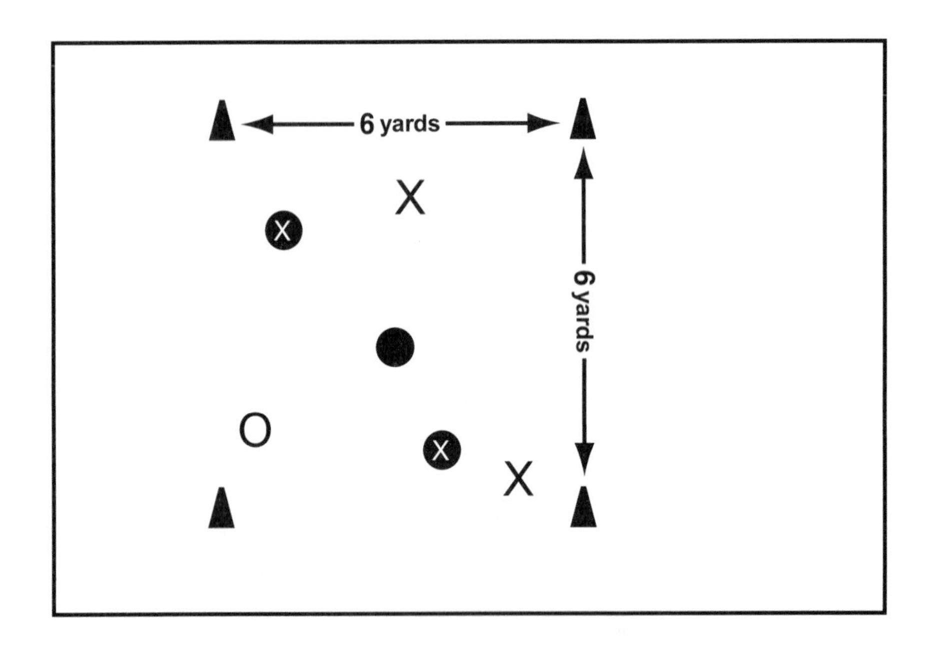

INSTRUCTIONS:
- Organize players in a small grid area.
- Players pair up and move about freely within the designated area, passing the ball back and forth with their partner (use one ball per pair).

COACHING POINTS:
- Use this drill to force players into the habit of keeping their heads up while passing.

VARIATIONS:
- Drill may be modified to focus on any type of pass or kick.
- Drill may prohibit forward passes.
- Drill may crowd the grid area with additional pairs of players in order to make to make execution more difficult.

7 SQUARE PASS

OBJECTIVE: Improving passing skills
NUMBER OF PLAYERS: 4
AREA/FIELD: 5 yards × 5 yards
TIME: 5–8 minutes
EQUIPMENT: 1 ball (per group)

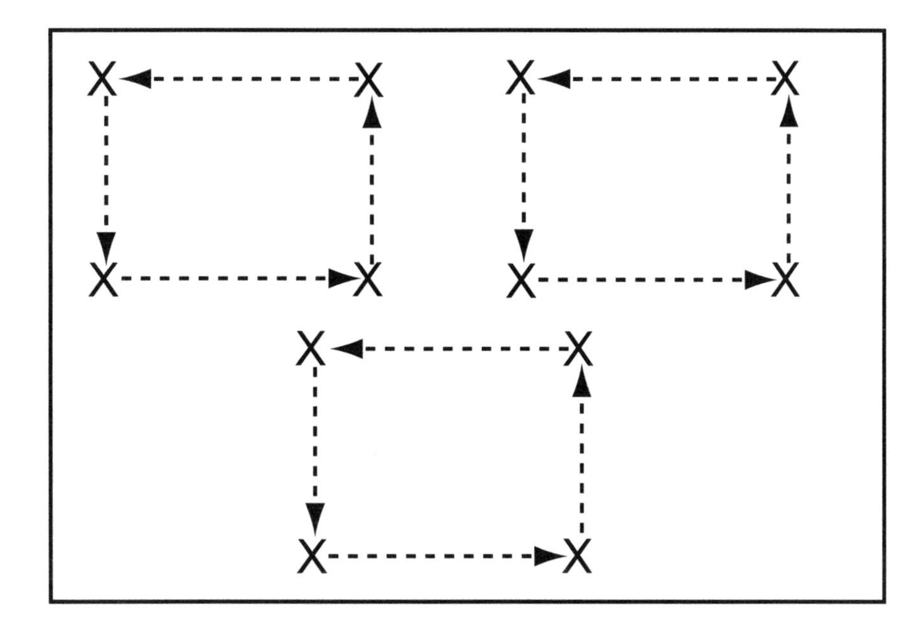

INSTRUCTIONS:
- Organize groups of players in square formations.
- Players face the center of the square and pass the ball around the square.

COACHING POINTS:
- Players should practice all types of passes; they should even practice handling bad passes.

VARIATIONS:
- Drill may require that players perform exercises between passes (when exercising, a player should face out rather than toward the center of the square).

8 IN BETWEEN

OBJECTIVE: Improving passing skills

NUMBER OF PLAYERS: 3

AREA/FIELD: 12 yards × 12 yards

TIME: 7–10 minutes

EQUIPMENT: 1 ball (per group), 2 pylons

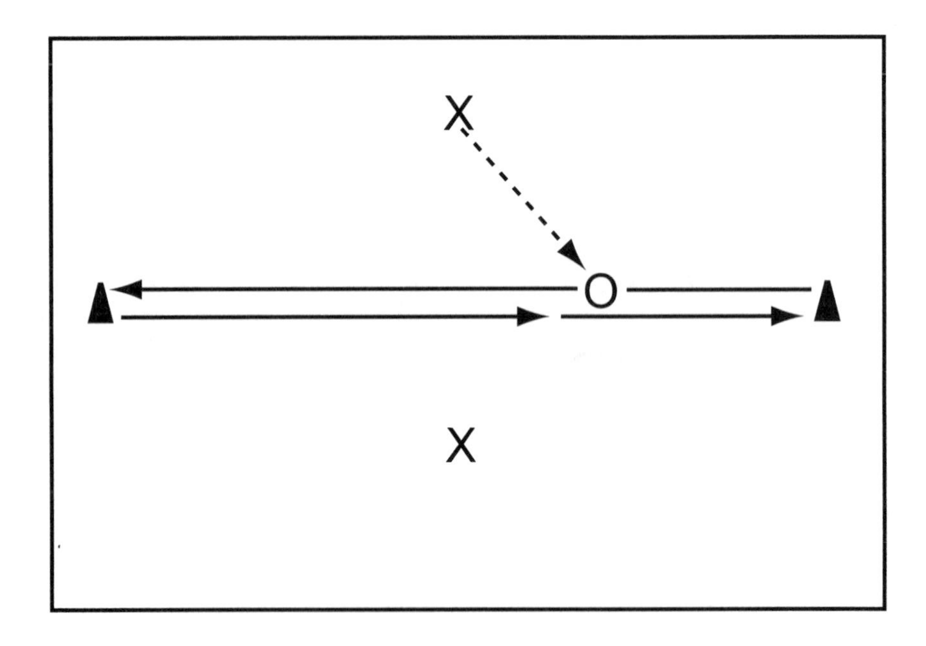

INSTRUCTIONS:

- Organize players according to the diagram above.
- A moving player runs back and forth between two stationary players, catching and passing a single ball back and forth between them.
- The moving player must catch and pass the ball quickly; this player runs approximately 6 meters following each pass.

COACHING POINTS:

- Drill works well if set up between the touch line and the 15-meter line.

VARIATIONS:

- The two passers may vary the pass in order to make it more difficult to catch.

9 PAIRS LOOP

OBJECTIVE: Improving passing skills
NUMBER OF PLAYERS: 8 (and up)
AREA/FIELD: Full field
TIME: 7–10 minutes
EQUIPMENT: 1 ball (per pair)

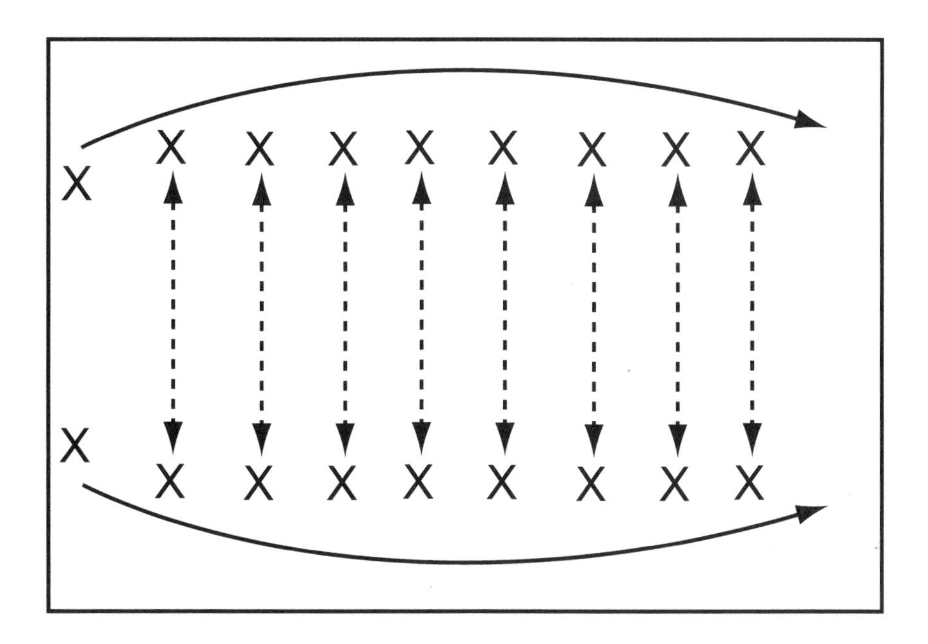

INSTRUCTIONS:

- Organize players in single-file lines facing across from one another.
- Players pair up with the person across from them, passing continuously.
- The front pair loops to the outside and runs to the back of the group.

VARIATIONS:

- On their way to the back, runners may move through the middle of the group; passing partners are forced to use a variety of passes to avoid hitting runners.

10 FIGURE 8'S

OBJECTIVE: Improving passing skills
NUMBER OF PLAYERS: 12–20
AREA/FIELD: 25 yards × 25 yards
TIME: 10 minutes
EQUIPMENT: 2 balls

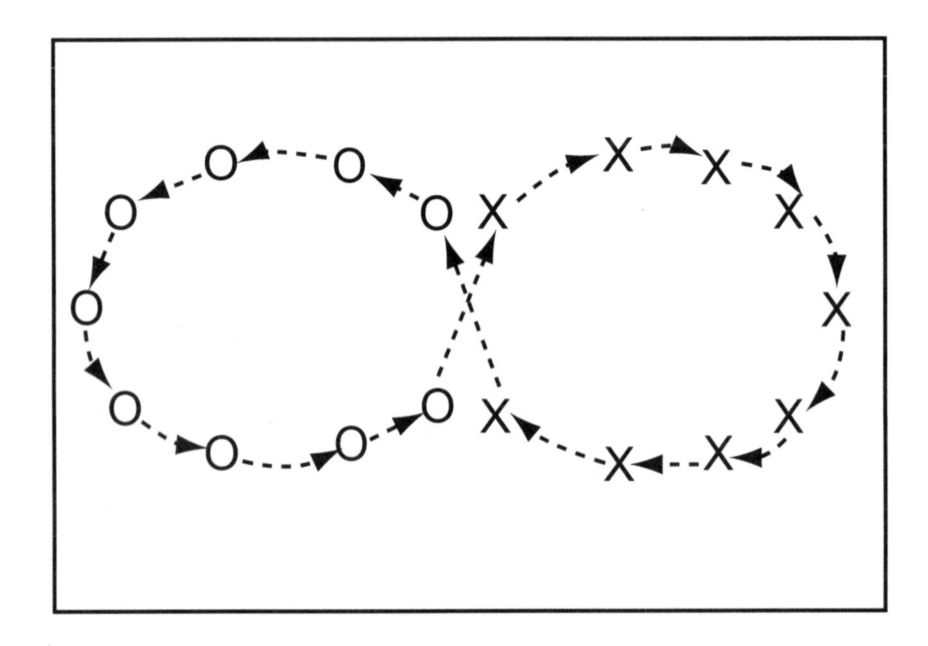

INSTRUCTIONS:

- Organize players in two teams in a circle formation; align circles side by side.
- Players practice passing the ball around each circle (one ball per circle).
- When the ball reaches the last person in the circle, that player passes the ball over to the first player in the adjoining circle.
- Each circle of players attempts to pass the ball around quickly so that one circle ends up with both balls.
- A team scores one point every time it ends up the winner (no ball in the circle); teams can compete to see who is the first to reach a specific point total.

COACHING POINTS:

- An excellent drill to encourage friendly competition.

11 CIRCLE

OBJECTIVE: Improving passing skills
NUMBER OF PLAYERS: 10 (and up)
AREA/FIELD: Half field
TIME: 7–10 minutes
EQUIPMENT: 1 ball

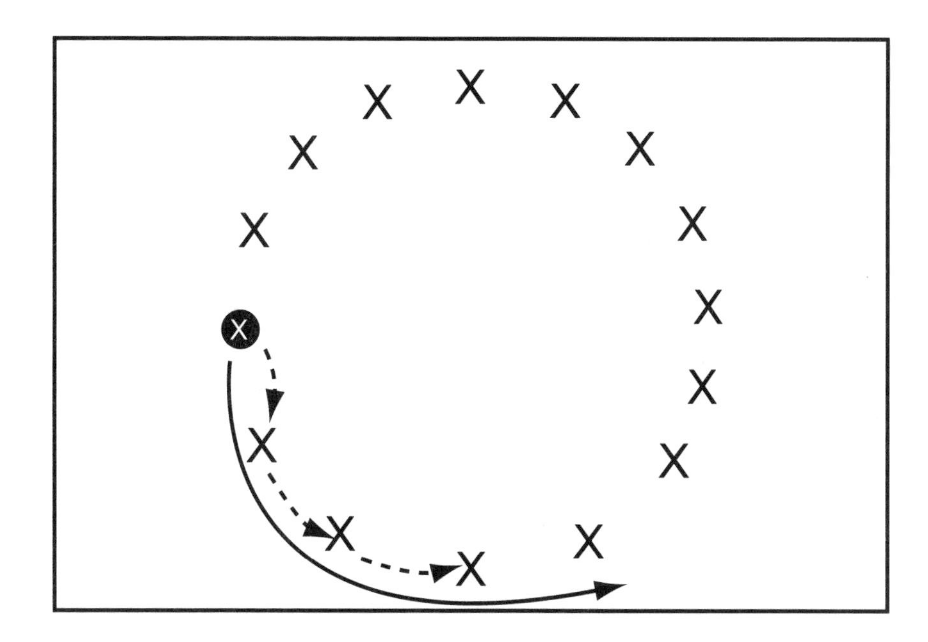

INSTRUCTIONS:
- Players pass the ball around the circle.
- One player races the ball completely around the circle, coming back to the spot originally occupied.
- The next player in line then attempts to beat the ball around the circle.

VARIATIONS:
- A player may attempt to beat the ball running backward around the circle.

12 5 TO 1

OBJECTIVE: Improving passing skills
NUMBER OF PLAYERS: 5
AREA/FIELD: Half field
TIME: 8 minutes
EQUIPMENT: 1 ball (per group)

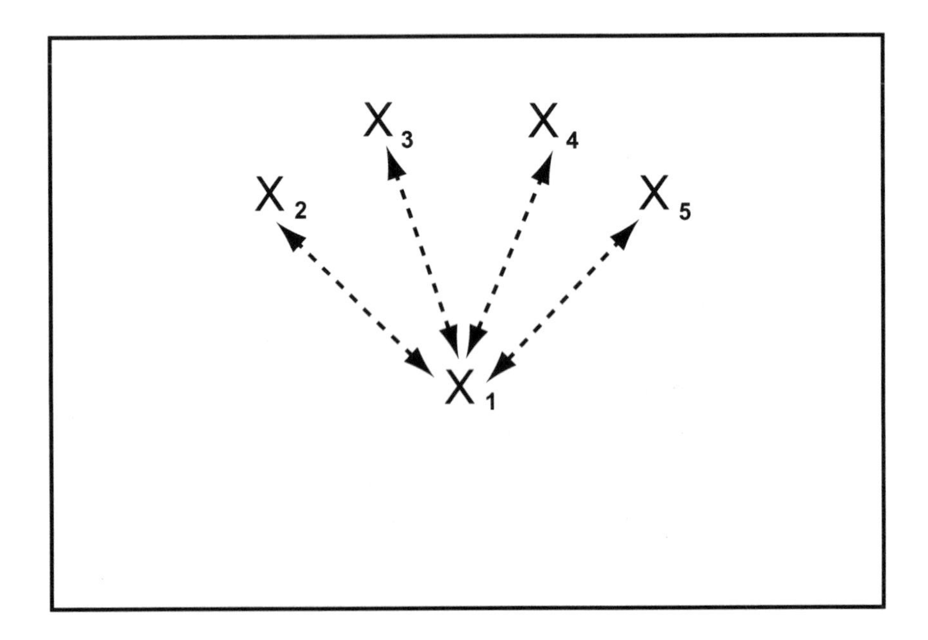

INSTRUCTIONS:

- A player with a ball stands facing four others arranged in a staggered or straight line.
- The single player passes the ball back and forth to each of the other four in the group.
- The group of players moves about the field by jogging forward; the single player must keep up while jogging backward.
- Once each player in the group has touched the ball the single player decks the ball.
- The single player then joins the group and one of the other players switches to the single position.

VARIATIONS:

- Players may move about the field in any direction while in this formation.

13 PRESSURE PASS/ QUICK HANDS

OBJECTIVE:	Improving passing skills (under pressure)
NUMBER OF PLAYERS:	8–10
AREA/FIELD:	Half field
TIME:	7–10 minutes
EQUIPMENT:	4 balls

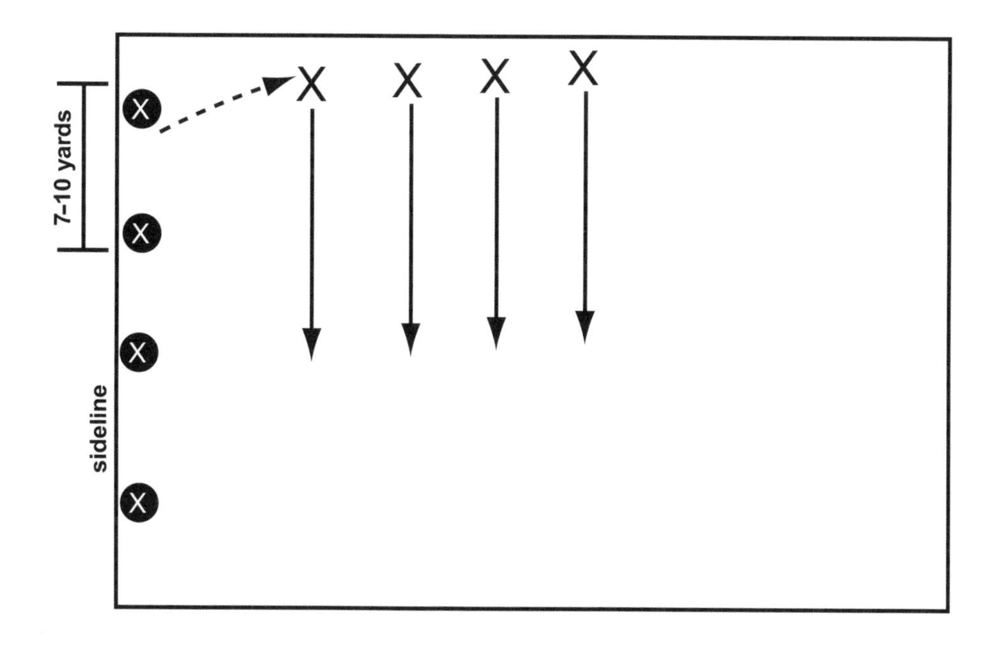

INSTRUCTIONS:

- Organize one group of passers along the sideline of the field (each with a ball) and another group of receivers in a single-file line facing across the field.
- Receivers wait their turn in line to run across the field, receiving/passing each of the balls from the stationary passers.
- The last player to catch the ball simply places it on the ground; the stationary passer chases/collects the ball and realigns for the next group.

VARIATIONS:

- A token defender may be added to chase after the balls while they are being passed.

14 THE CHASE

OBJECTIVE: Improving passing skills (under pressure)
NUMBER OF PLAYERS: 4–6
AREA/FIELD: Half (up to full field)
TIME: 7 minutes
EQUIPMENT: 1 ball (per group)

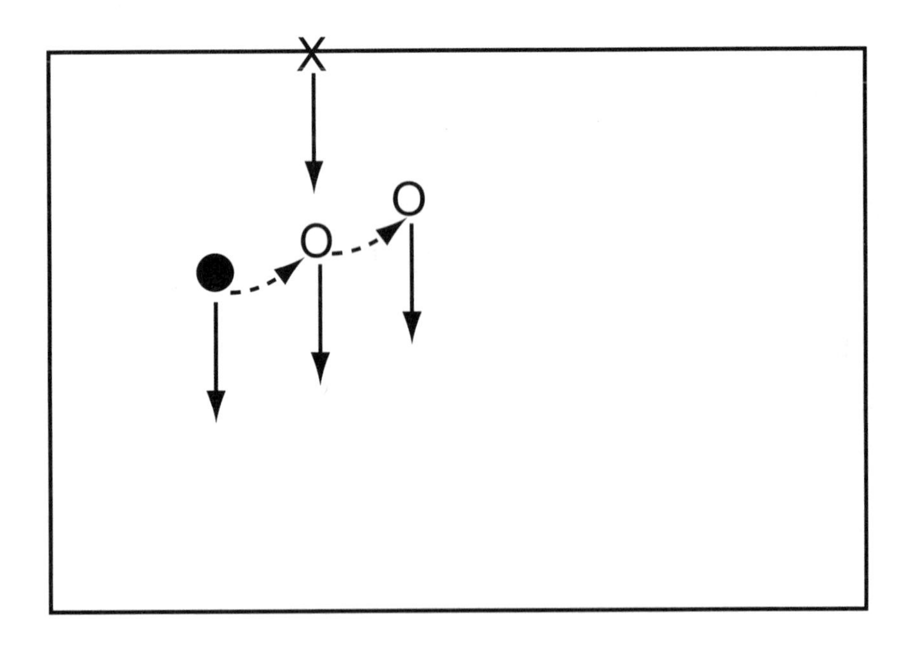

INSTRUCTIONS:

- Three players run and pass the ball as fast as they can until they reach the goal line.
- A fourth player, who starts on the goal line, chases the other three.
- None of the passers can run with their hands on the ball for more than 3 meters.

15 BACK AND FORTH

OBJECTIVE: Improving passing skills (under pressure)
NUMBER OF PLAYERS: Groups of 4
AREA/FIELD: 30 yards × 30 yards
TIME: 10 minutes
EQUIPMENT: 1 ball (per group)

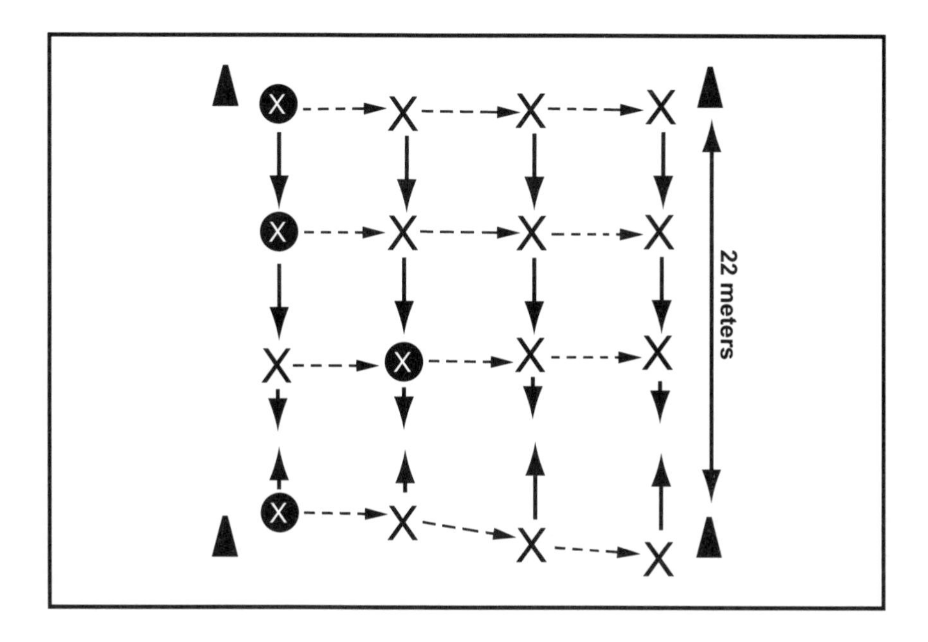

INSTRUCTIONS:

- Organize players in single-file lines.
- The first players in each line form a group and pass the ball along between them.
- Each group runs continuously between lines on the field while passing.
- This drill is commonly carried out between the goal line and the 22-meter line.

COACHING POINTS:

- With multiple groups running and passing at the same time, players must concentrate on passing the ball within their own group.

16 11 VS. 3

OBJECTIVE: Improving passing skills (under pressure)
NUMBER OF PLAYERS: 14
AREA/FIELD: 50 yards × 50 yards
TIME: 10 minutes
EQUIPMENT: 1 ball, 4 pylons

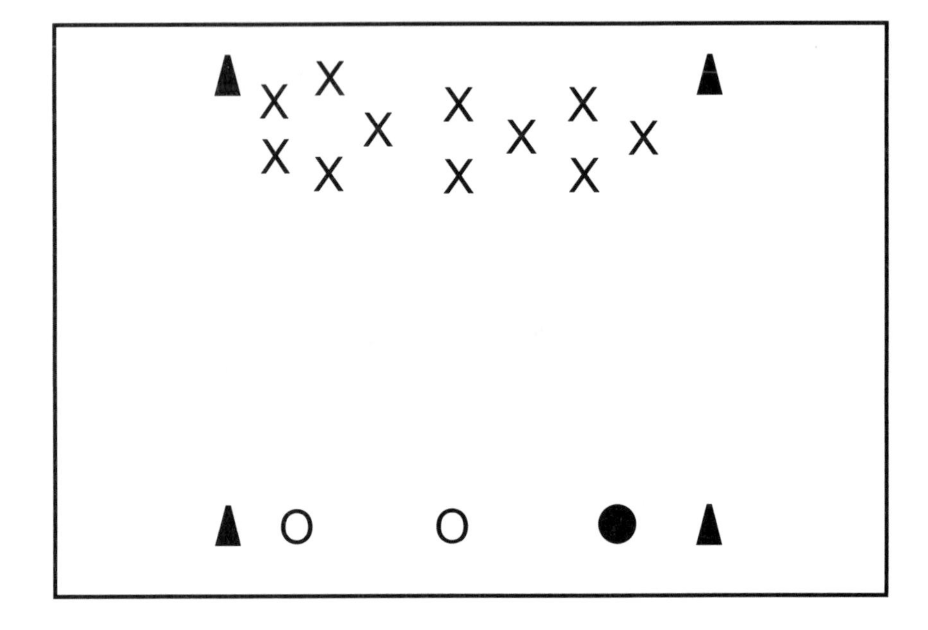

INSTRUCTIONS:

- Organize players into two teams—11 versus 3.
- Team of 3 kicks off from their own goal line to the team of 11.
- The larger team attempts to score by taking the ball over the goal line.
- The shorthanded team is allowed to run full speed, while the larger team must walk.
- Tackling is replaced with a touch rule: any player who is touched while in possession of the ball must rotate onto the short-sided team and switch positions with the "toucher."

17 ALL AGAINST ONE

OBJECTIVE: Improving passing skills (under pressure)
NUMBER OF PLAYERS: 8–10
AREA/FIELD: 15 yards × 15 yards
TIME: 10 minutes
EQUIPMENT: 1 ball, 4 pylons

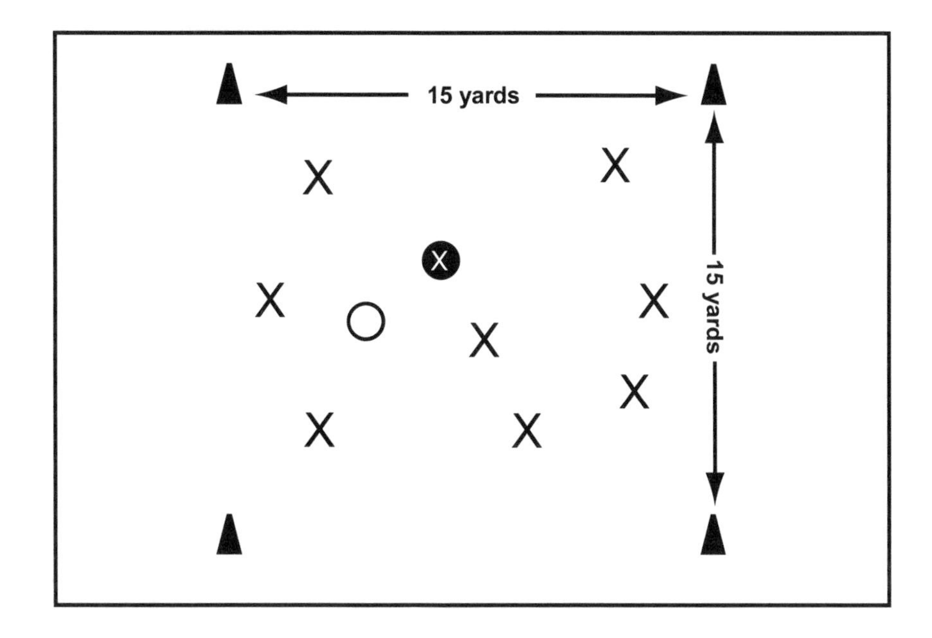

INSTRUCTIONS:

- Organize up to 10 players in a grid area.
- A player acts as a runner while all other players pass the ball back and forth in an attempt to tag the runner with the ball.
- A fair tag is one in which the player tags the runner while maintaining possession of the ball.
- The runner can move anywhere inside the area; all other players can move anywhere in the area unless in possession of the ball (at which point they cannot move).

18 TRIANGLE BALL

OBJECTIVE: Improving passing skills and pass support
NUMBER OF PLAYERS: 4
AREA/FIELD: 10 yards × 10 yards
TIME: 5–8 minutes
EQUIPMENT: 1 ball, 4 pylons

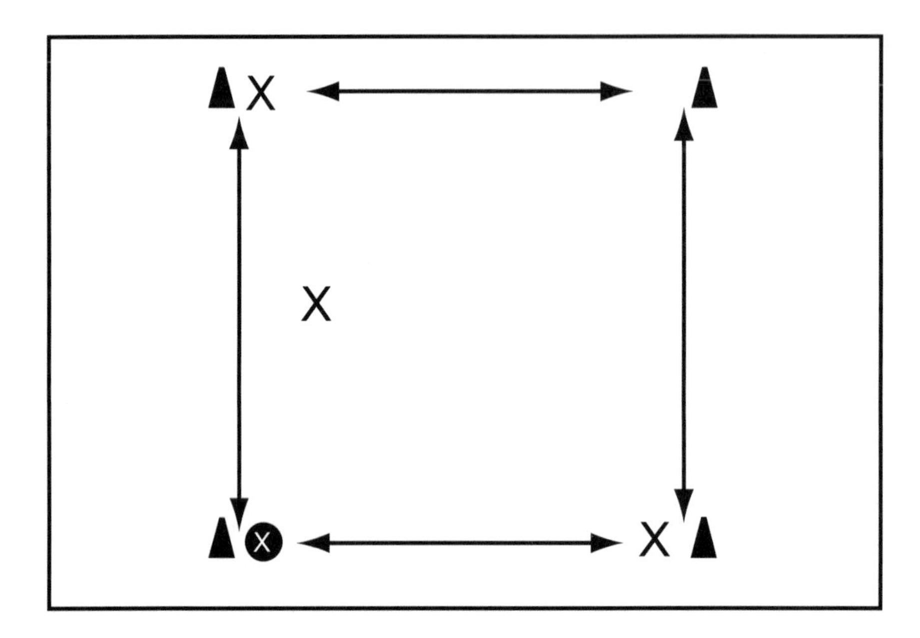

INSTRUCTIONS:

- Organize players in a square area.
- Three players work on the corners and sides.
- A player in the center of the square attempts to intercept the ball as the others pass it.
- The outside three players can only pass and run along the sides of the square (they cannot pass diagonally).
- Players on the outside cannot move once they receive a pass (teammates should support them on either side).
- If a pass is intercepted or knocked down, the center player moves to the corner/sides of the square (the player who made the bad pass moves to the center).

19 ORDER BALL

OBJECTIVE: Improving passing skills and pass support

NUMBER OF PLAYERS: 4–6

AREA/FIELD: Half field

TIME: 7–10 minutes

EQUIPMENT: 1 ball (per group)

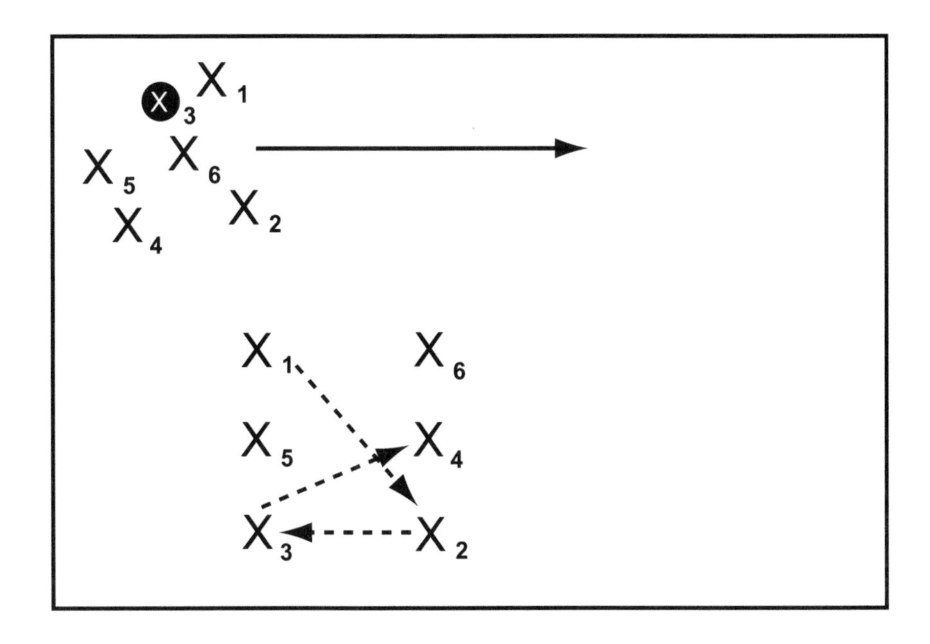

INSTRUCTIONS:

- Organize teams in formation (players may be arranged in lines, circles, or moving groups).
- Players are assigned designated numbers and move around the field attempting to pass the ball back and forth in numeric order.

VARIATIONS:

- Drill may be modified to focus on additional skills besides passing (i.e., kicking, decking the ball, etc.).

20 PATTERN BALL

OBJECTIVE: Improving passing skills and pass support

NUMBER OF PLAYERS: 6

AREA/FIELD: Half field

TIME: 7–10 minutes

EQUIPMENT: 1 ball (per line)

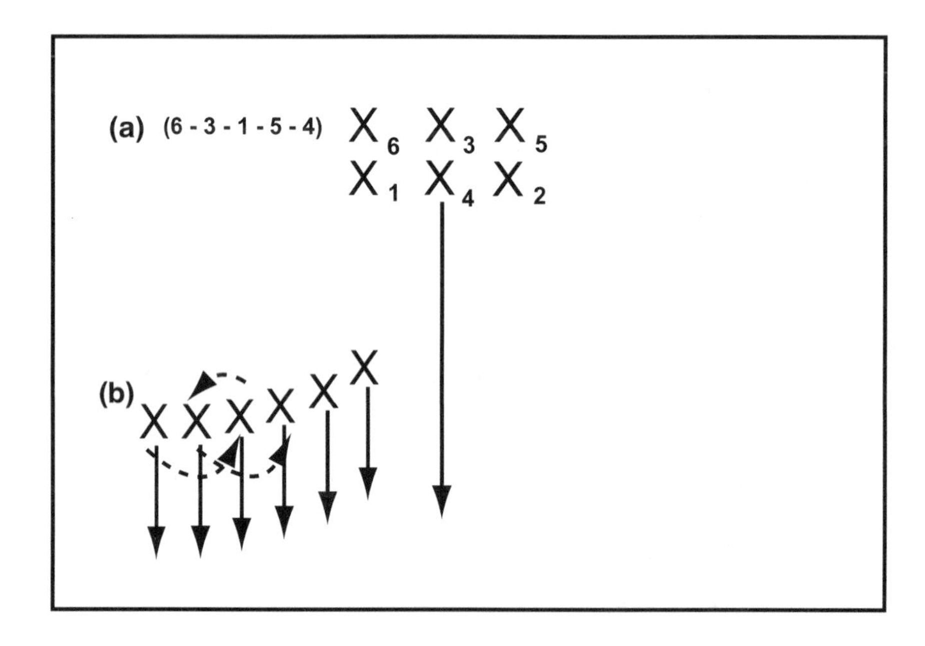

INSTRUCTIONS:

- Organize players in lines or groups.
- Players move across the field passing the ball back and forth.

a) Players may be assigned designated numbers and attempt to pass and receive the ball in a specified order (the coach should set the numbered order—i.e., 6-3-1-5-4-2).

b) Players may attempt to pass the ball to the second player outside them, and then that player passes back inside (the pattern is skip one player then pass back inside to the skipped player, etc.)

COACHING POINTS:

- Players should run hard onto the pass and support from depth.

21 TOUCH RUGBY

OBJECTIVE: Improving passing skills and pass support
NUMBER OF PLAYERS: 8–20
AREA/FIELD: Half field
TIME: 10–20 minutes
EQUIPMENT: 1 ball

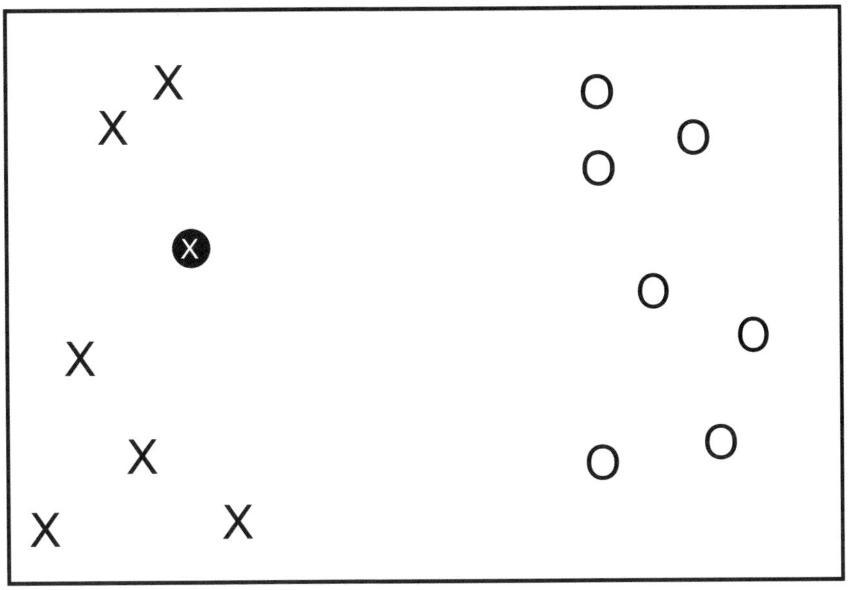

INSTRUCTIONS:

- Organize players into two teams of equal numbers.
- Play begins with a kickoff by one team; the other team attempts to run the ball back and score on the opposition.
- The offensive team is given a set number of chances to score (the number of chances is often three, but this number can be changed).
- When a player in possession of the ball is touched, the player's team loses a chance; when all chances are gone, the ball is given over to the opposing team.
- When touched, a player must stop moving and restart play by tapping the ball forward from the ground and then passing it.

- The opposition must back up 5 meters from the "mark" where the ball is downed; once the ball is tapped, the opposition may move forward.
- Standard rugby rules apply regarding offsides, passing, etc. (i.e., if a forward pass occurs, the other team gains possession of the ball).
- If the ball is dropped forward during play, the other team gains possession.
- Intercepts are permitted as long as the player is onside.
- Kicking is not permitted during the game.
- A score occurs when the ball is run across the goal line and touched to the ground before a defensive player touches the attacking player; if a player is touched in the goal area before tapping the ball, play restarts on the 5-meter line.
- After a score, the teams switch attacking/defending roles; play restarts with a kickoff (the former attacking team kicks off to the former defending team).

COACHING POINTS:

- Encourage quick play.
- Ensure that the defensive team gives the full 5-meter space following touches.
- Use the drill as an effective warm-up game before practice.

22 WINDOW BALL

OBJECTIVE: Improving passing and catching skills

NUMBER OF PLAYERS: 2–10

AREA/FIELD: 15 yards × 15 yards

TIME: 8–10 minutes

EQUIPMENT: 1 ball

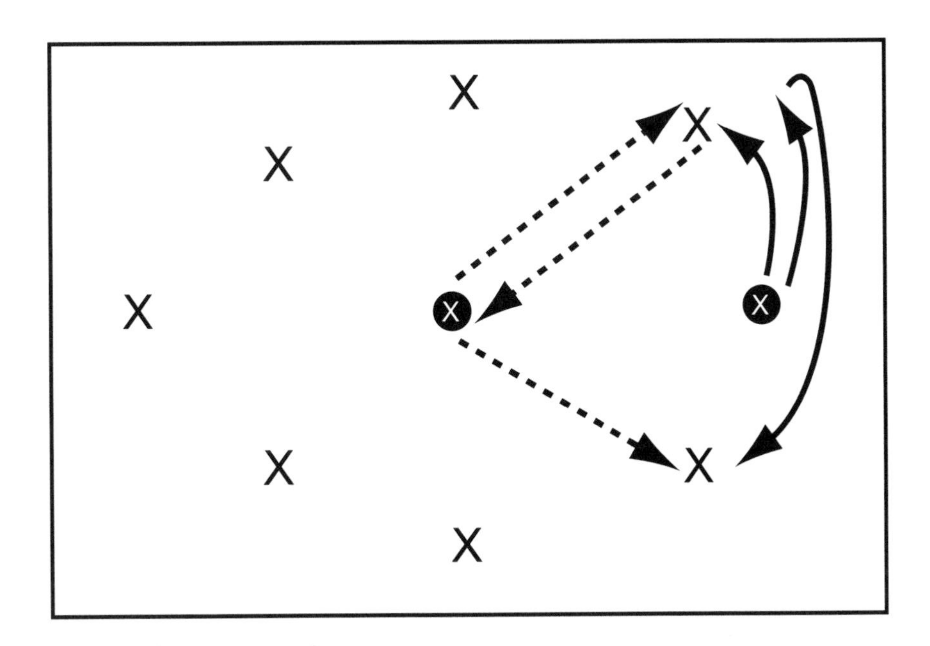

INSTRUCTIONS:

- Organize players in a circle formation with a passer in the center and a runner on the outside.
- The runner goes backward a position in the circle, then receives/gives a pass from/to the passer.
- The runner then runs forward two spaces and receives/gives a pass (this process is repeated until the runner returns to the original spot).
- The passer then takes the runner's place, the runner joins the circle, and a new player takes over as passer.

COACHING POINTS:

- Players should move quickly while keeping hands up as targets.

VARIATIONS:

- Drill may be executed using pylons as replacements for players other than runner and passer.

23 CORNER BALL

OBJECTIVE: Improving passing skills and movement without the ball

NUMBER OF PLAYERS: 8–16

AREA/FIELD: 15 yards × 15 yards

TIME: 7–10 minutes

EQUIPMENT: 1 ball, 4 pylons

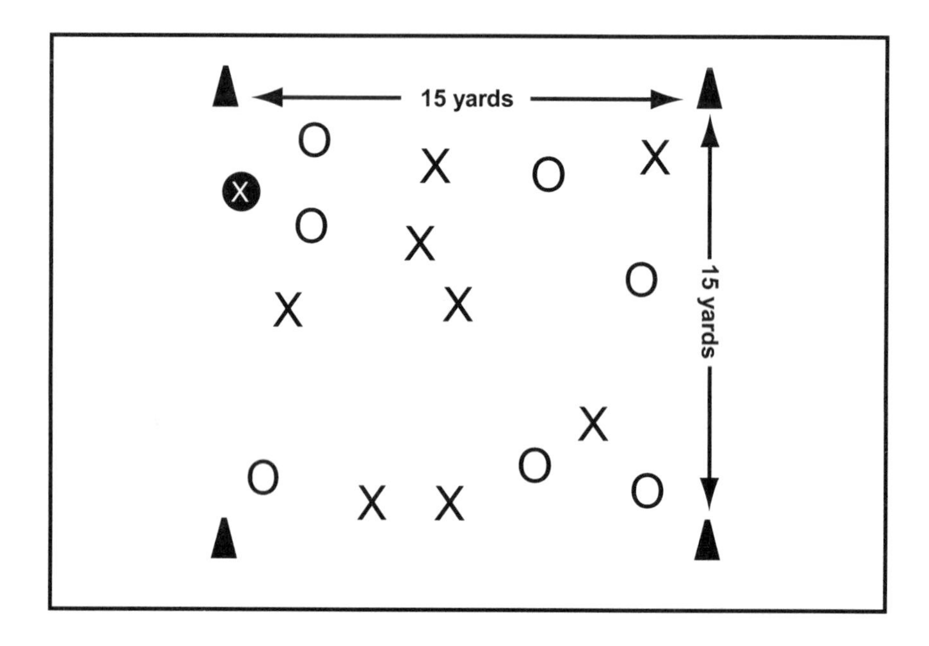

INSTRUCTIONS:

- Organize two equal-numbered teams in a grid area.
- An attacking team with possession of the ball attempts to tag runners on the other team one by one.
- A fair tag involves tagging the runner with the ball while maintaining possession of the ball; if the ball is dropped, the opposing team gains possession.
- Players can move anywhere within the grid area until gaining possession of the ball (at which point a player cannot move).

COACHING POINTS:

- Passer and receiver should make eye contact.
- Emphasize teamwork and communication.

VARIATIONS:

- Tagged players may be required to perform a conditioning exercise.

24 MIDDLE RUN

OBJECTIVE: Improving passing skills and speed
NUMBER OF PLAYERS: 7
AREA/FIELD: 40 yards × 40 yards
TIME: 7–10 minutes
EQUIPMENT: 1 ball

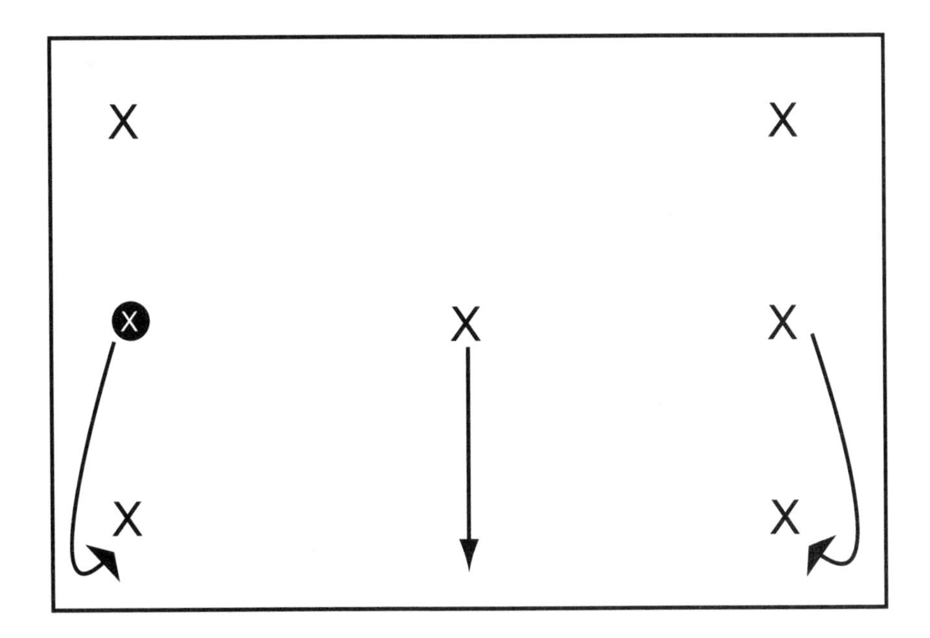

INSTRUCTIONS:

- Organize players according to the diagram above.
- One ball goes with the three.
- The two players outside the runners drop off and the two at the other end join the middle runner and go back the opposite way.
- This process is repeated for a set time or set number of runs; the middle runner changes with one of the other players.
- The group attempts to see how many times they can pass the ball among themselves before they get to the end.

25 OPPOSITES

OBJECTIVE: Improving passing skills and fitness

NUMBER OF PLAYERS: 8

AREA/FIELD: 20 yards × 20 yards

TIME: 7 minutes

EQUIPMENT: 2 balls

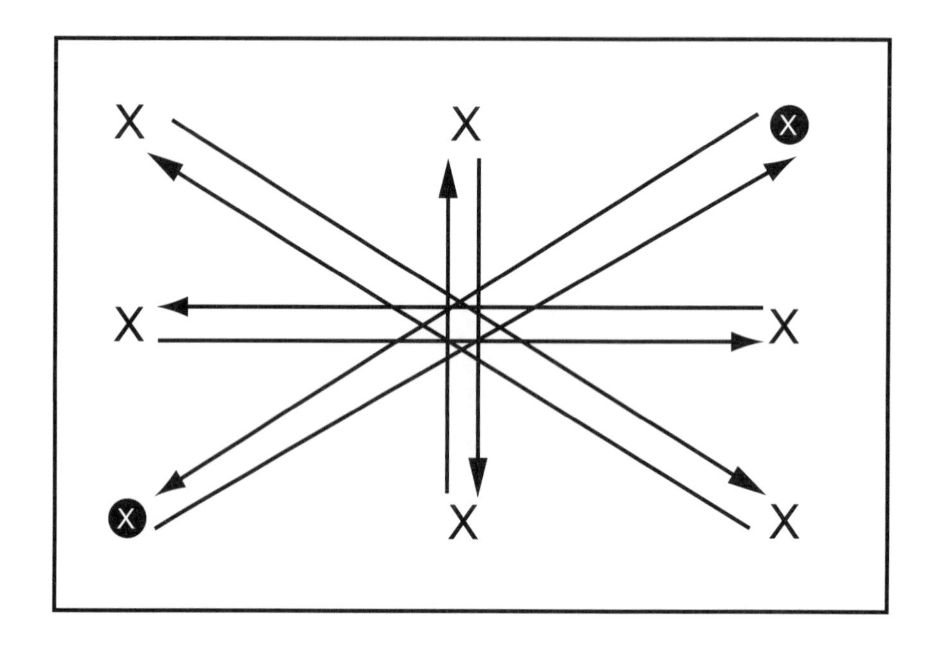

INSTRUCTIONS:

- Organize players in a square formation.
- Players begin to pass two balls (from opposite corners); balls must be passed in the same direction.
- Players who have the ball pass it to the person on the right and then run to the position directly opposite on the square.

26 LINE PASSING

OBJECTIVE: Improving backline passing skills
NUMBER OF PLAYERS: Groups of 4–6
AREA/FIELD: Half field
TIME: 10–15 minutes
EQUIPMENT: 1 ball (per group)

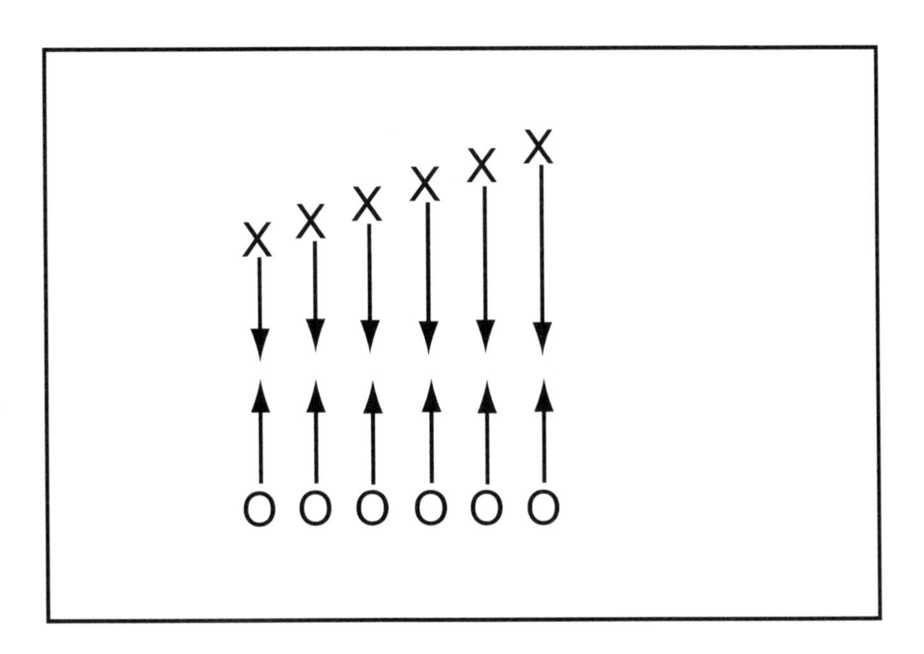

INSTRUCTIONS:
- Organize players in lines; players should be aligned side by side.
- Each group moves downfield, passing the ball in a variety of manners (i.e., straight or regular passes, low or high passes, miss one and back inside, miss one and loop, single-player loop, unit loop, scissors, switching, drifts, chip kicks, grubbers, etc.).

COACHING POINTS:
- Virtually any back movement can be practiced in this drill setting.

VARIATIONS:
- Drill may be run against full opposition or token opposition, against the blocking bags, or unopposed.
- Refer to Chapter 5, "Back Play," for a variety of alternatives.

27 SCRUM HALF PASS

OBJECTIVE: Improving scrum half passing skills
NUMBER OF PLAYERS: 2
AREA/FIELD: Half field
TIME: 5–7 minutes
EQUIPMENT: 1 ball

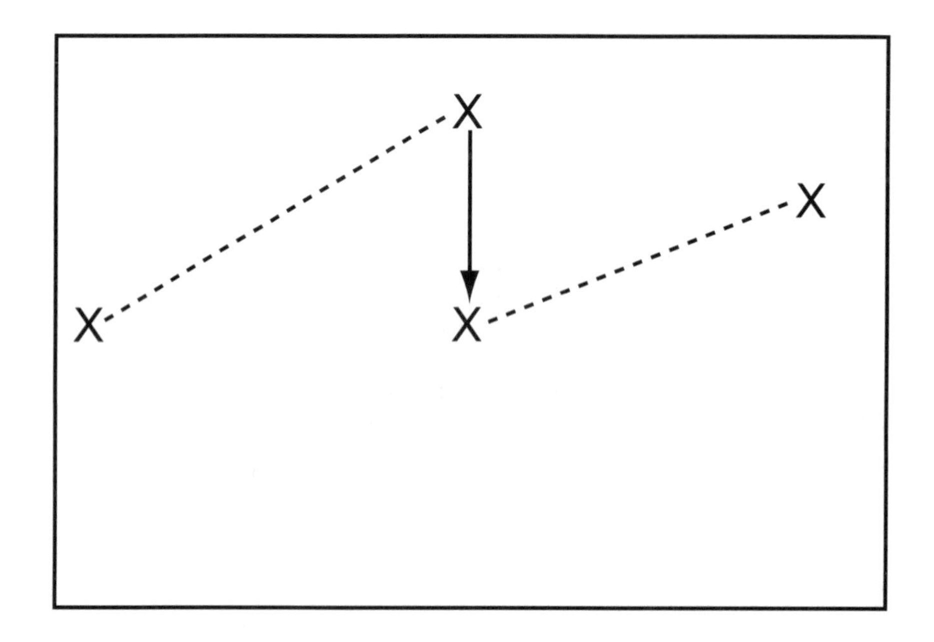

INSTRUCTIONS:

- Organize players according to the diagram above.
- Drill involves two players: scrum half and receiver.
- The scrum half player performs continuous passes.
- The receiver returns the ball after a brief run.

COACHING POINTS:

- Scrum half players should be drilled on this type of passing at every practice session.

VARIATIONS:

- Drill may be set to work passes in both directions.
- Drill may involve varying the type of passing and the manner in which the scrum half receives the ball.
- The ball can be decked when caught, with realignment taking place from that spot.

28 BALL TAG

OBJECTIVE: Improving passing skills and team play

NUMBER OF PLAYERS: 8–14

AREA/FIELD: 15 yards × 15 yards

TIME: 10–15 minutes

EQUIPMENT: 1 ball (per group), 4 pylons

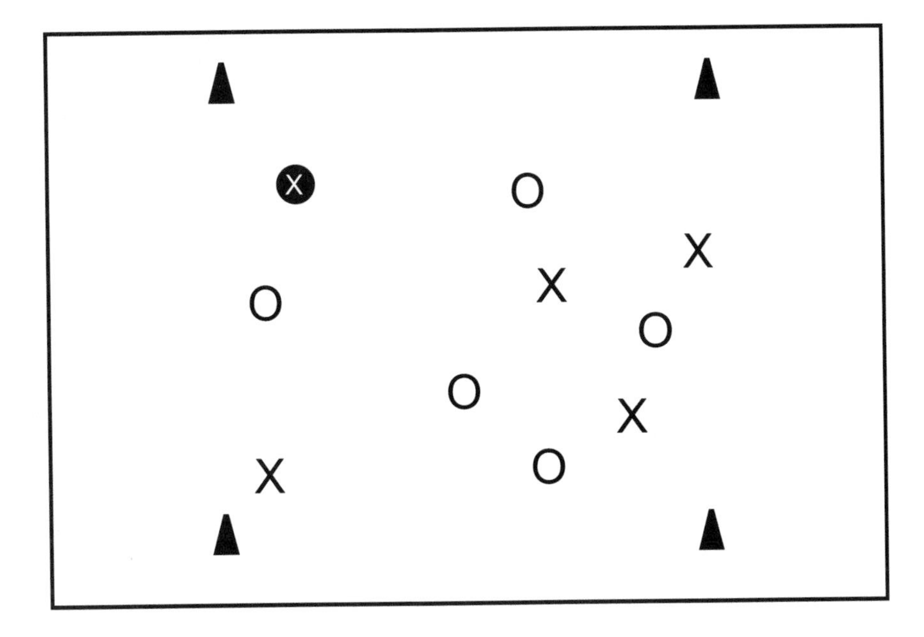

INSTRUCTIONS:

- Organize two teams in a grid area.
- An attacking team attempts to eliminate a defending team by tagging opposing players with the ball.
- The attacking (tagging) team players may move anywhere within the grid area until in possession of the ball (at which point that player cannot move).
- The defending team cannot interfere with the passing of the ball by the attacking team and attempts to avoid being tagged.
- A player is eliminated from the game when tagged.
- If the ball is dropped, players return to the group in reverse order of their elimination.
- When all players are eliminated, the attacking and defending teams switch roles.

COACHING POINTS:

- Drill serves as an excellent fitness drill.

VARIATIONS:

- Tagged players may be required to perform a conditioning exercise.

29 END BALL

OBJECTIVE: Improving passing skills and team play

NUMBER OF PLAYERS: 10–16

AREA/FIELD: 15 × 15 yards (up to half field)

TIME: 10–15 minutes

EQUIPMENT: 1 ball, 8 pylons

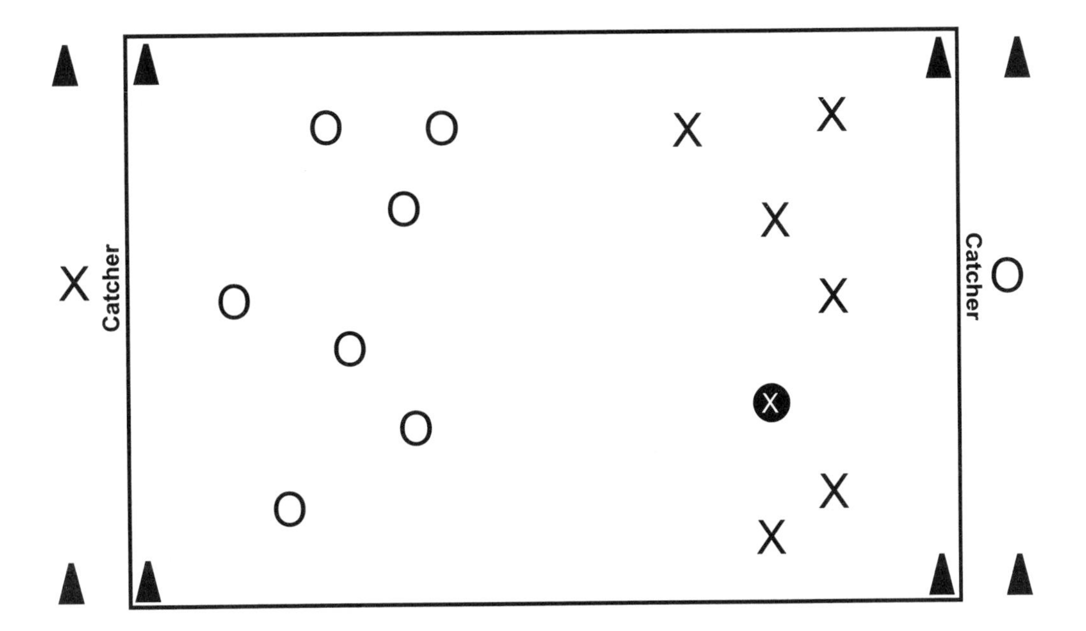

INSTRUCTIONS:

- Organize two teams in a grid area (adjust grid size according to the number of players).
- Attempt to pass the ball over the end line to a designated teammate, who touches the ball to the ground.
- Players in possession of the ball cannot run with it (opposition coverage is similar to that of basketball).
- Once a player touches the ball, the opposition must allow a meter area in which to move the ball (no contact is permitted).
- A ball that is dropped or knocked down goes over to the opposition.
- The opposition gets immediate possession of the ball following a score.

COACHING POINTS:

- Players should continue to move when not in possession of the ball.
- Emphasize effective communication with teammates.

VARIATIONS:

- A defender may be added within the goal area to cover the catcher.

30 MAT BALL

OBJECTIVE: Improving passing skills and team play

NUMBER OF PLAYERS: 14–20

AREA/FIELD: 40 yards × 40 yards

TIME: 15–20 minutes

EQUIPMENT: 1 ball, 2 mats, 4 pylons

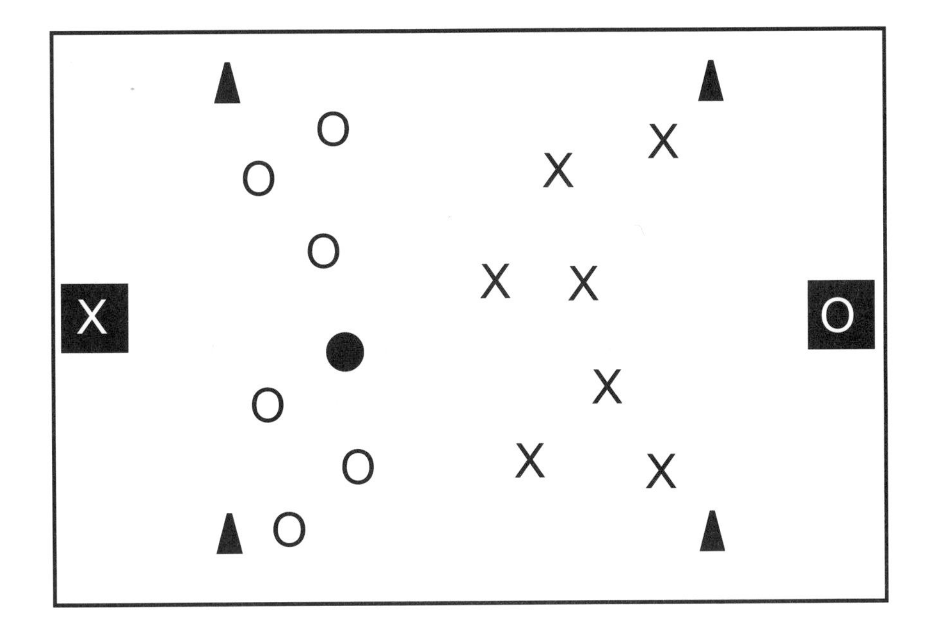

INSTRUCTIONS:

- Organize two teams in a grid area.
- Players attempt to score by passing the ball to a teammate (catcher) located on a 4 × 4 mat in the opposition's end of the field.
- The designated catcher is the only player permitted on the mat; defenders cannot make contact with the catcher or the mat area.
- Defenders attempt to tag the offensive player in possession of the ball.
- A tagged player cannot run with the ball but must instead pass it (opposition coverage is similar to that in basketball).
- A dropped ball results in a turnover.

VARIATIONS:

- Drill may allow standing tackles for coverage and allow one player to come in and rip the ball from teammate in possession.
- Drill may allow full tackles and permit players to support the play.
- Drill may require passes to be backward once over center.
- Drill may be executed using pylons as replacements for mats.

31 IN CLOSE AND OUT WIDE

OBJECTIVE: Improving passing skills and team communication

NUMBER OF PLAYERS: 2

AREA/FIELD: Half field

TIME: 5 minutes

EQUIPMENT: 1 ball

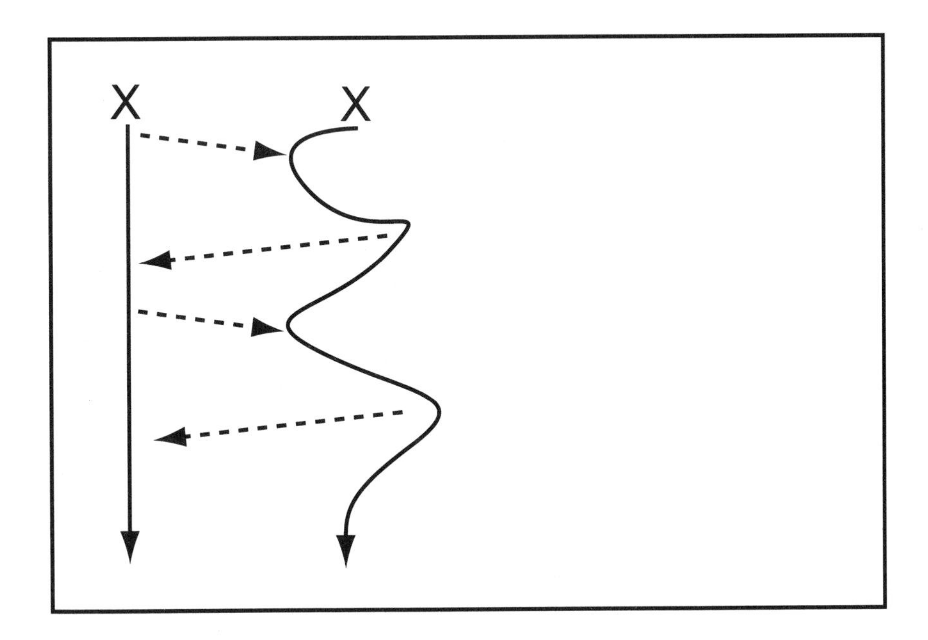

INSTRUCTIONS:
- Organize players so that they are lined up across from one another.
- While one player runs in a straight line, the other alternates between cutting in for a short pass and moving out for a wide pass.

COACHING POINTS:
- Players should support from depth.

VARIATIONS:
- The player running straight may choose to call for a short or wide pass.

32 LINE RELAYS

OBJECTIVE: Improving various skills
NUMBER OF PLAYERS: 4–6 (per group)
AREA/FIELD: Half field
TIME: 10–15 minutes
EQUIPMENT: 1 ball (per group)

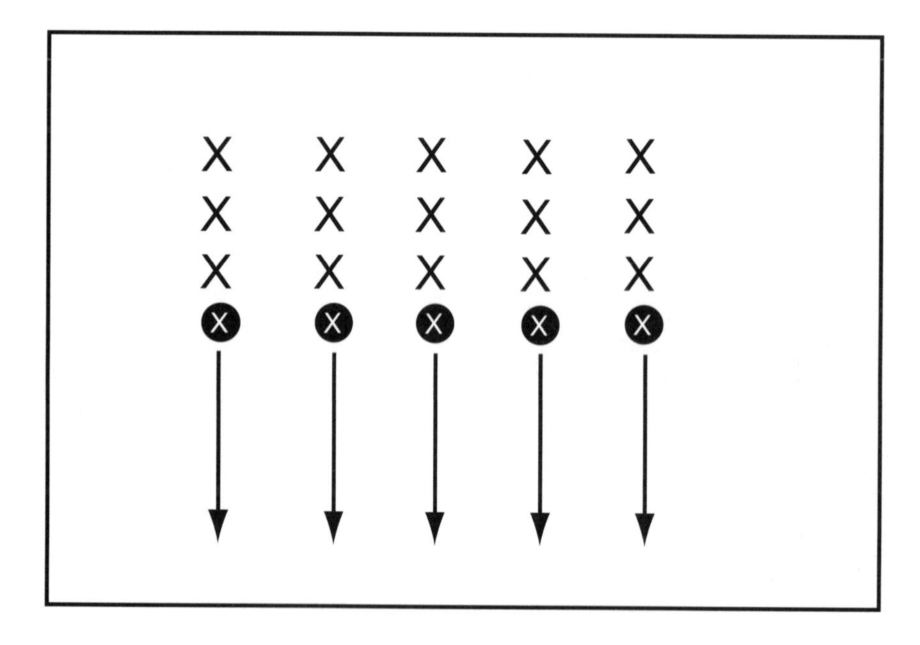

INSTRUCTIONS:

- Organize players in single-file lines.
- The player at the front of each line is given a ball and required to perform various tasks (i.e., roll the ball out, slide on it and return, chip kick, grub kick and chase, touch the ball down, return the ball to the player in the line with a handoff, pop pass, or deck the ball at the next player's feet).

COACHING POINTS:

- Drill can be run individually or the whole single-file line can travel up and down the field as a unit.

33 CRISSCROSS (NEW ZEALAND DRILL)

OBJECTIVE: Improving various skills

NUMBER OF PLAYERS: 8–20

AREA/FIELD: 20 yards × 20 yards

TIME: 10–15 minutes

EQUIPMENT: 2 balls

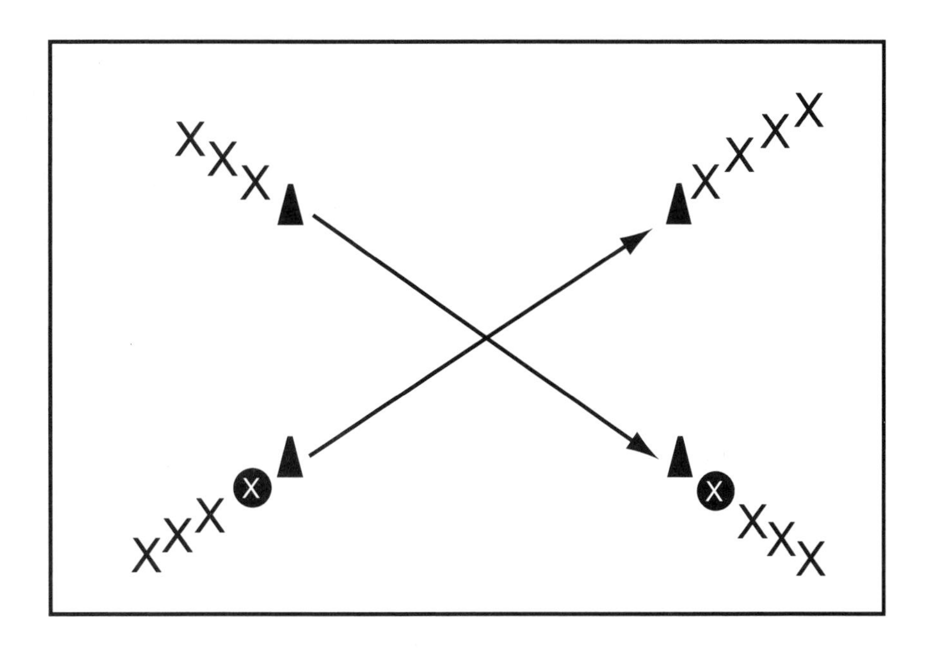

INSTRUCTIONS:

- Organize players in lines in opposite corners of a square formation.
- Start with a ball at the front of two lines; while facing diagonally toward the opposing corner, the first player in each of these lines runs toward the opposite corner and passes the ball to the waiting player in that line.
- Players may choose to exchange the ball in a variety of manners (i.e., handoffs, straight or regular passes, high or low passes, decking the ball a meter out, etc.).

COACHING POINTS:

- Drill is a favorite among players and coaches.

VARIATIONS:

- Players may use a single ball, time their runs (always passing to the left or right), and attempt to keep the ball suspended in a square-meter space, with each player transferring the ball somewhere close to the middle of the square.
- Players may use additional balls (such as one ball per line).
- Players may mix up the opposite corner rotation and move between lines in the following ways: run to the center, cut to the left or right, hand off to the left or right; pass to the left, run to the right; pass to the right, run to the left.

KICKING GAMES

34 KICKING CHALLENGE

OBJECTIVE: Improving kicking skills

NUMBER OF PLAYERS: 2

AREA/FIELD: Goal-line area

TIME: 7 minutes

EQUIPMENT: 1 ball, 1 goalpost upright

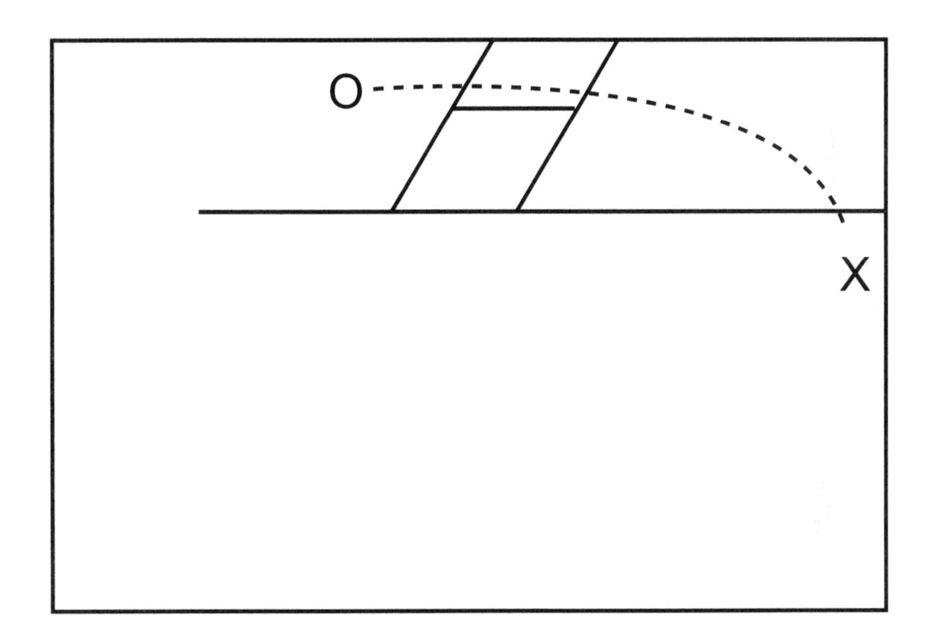

INSTRUCTIONS:

- A kicker lines up on the touch line, 5-meter line, or 15-meter line; this player is 5 meters from the goal line.
- A receiver lines up diagonally opposite the kicker.
- The kicker gets 1 point for a kick that crosses on the near side of the posts, 2 points for one that crosses on the far side of the posts, and 3 points for one through the uprights.

COACHING POINTS:

- Various kicks can be practiced in this drill.

35 UPRIGHTS

OBJECTIVE: Improving kicking skills

NUMBER OF PLAYERS: 6–20

AREA/FIELD: Half field

TIME: 10–15 minutes

EQUIPMENT: 1 ball, 8 pylons

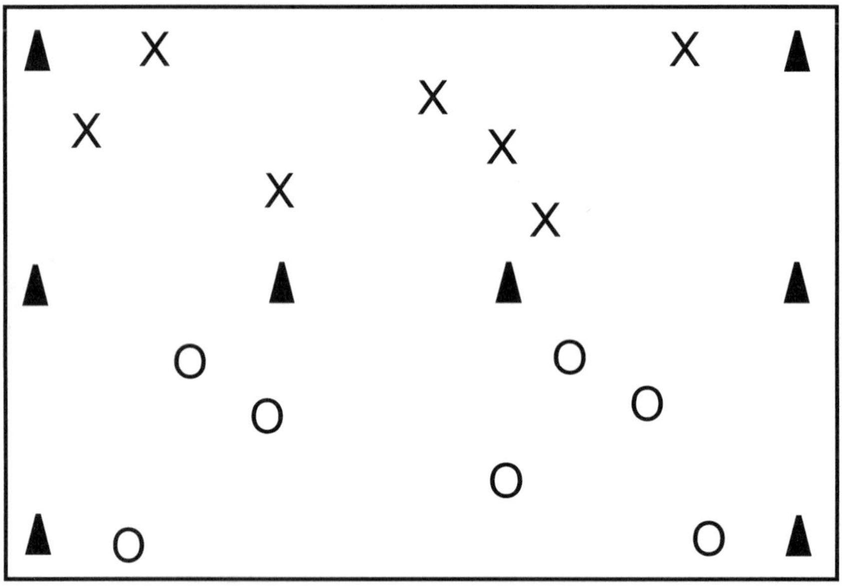

INSTRUCTIONS:

- Organize players into two teams of equal numbers and have each team spread out in a designated area (either on each side of the goalposts or on each side of a marked divider).
- Players attempt to kick the ball to open areas so that it lands in the opponent's area without the opponent catching it.
- Players take turns kicking.

36 5-ON-5 ACCURACY KICK

OBJECTIVE: Improving kicking skills
NUMBER OF PLAYERS: 6–10
AREA/FIELD: Half field (up to full field)
TIME: 10 minutes
EQUIPMENT: 1 ball, 4 pylons

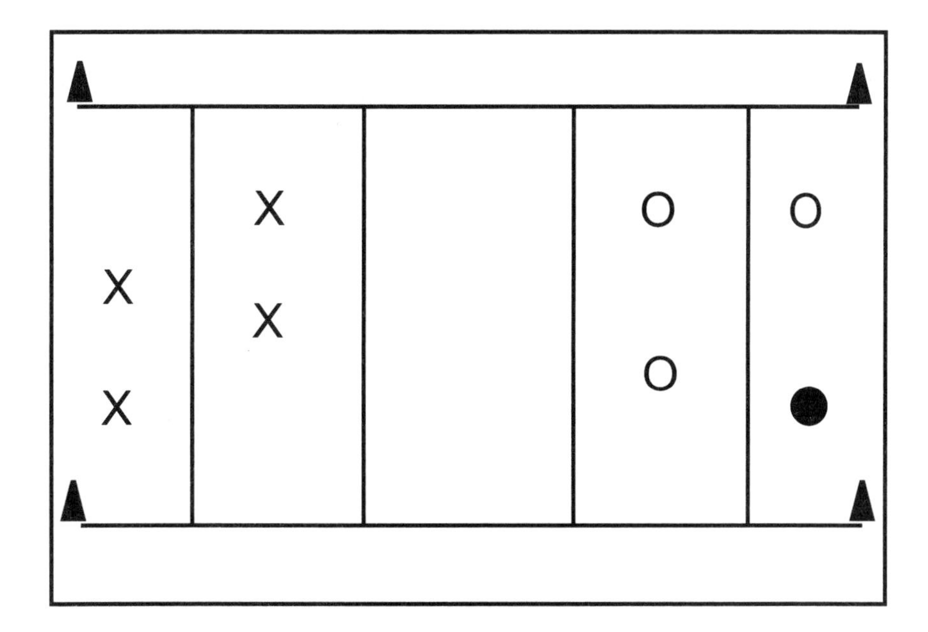

INSTRUCTIONS:

- Organize two teams of equal numbers on a field divided into five separate grid areas.
- The middle grid area (no-man's-land) is left empty; the teams, separated by the empty grid, occupy the areas at each end of the field.
- Players attempt to kick the ball so that it lands in the opponent's grid.
- Kicks that are caught cannot be kicked back until the ball has been passed twice.
- Each team starts with 10 points; a point is lost every time a team drops a ball or fails to land a ball in the opposition grid area.

37 TOUCH KICK

OBJECTIVE: Improving touch kicking

NUMBER OF PLAYERS: 2

AREA/FIELD: Half field

TIME: 10 minutes

EQUIPMENT: 1 ball

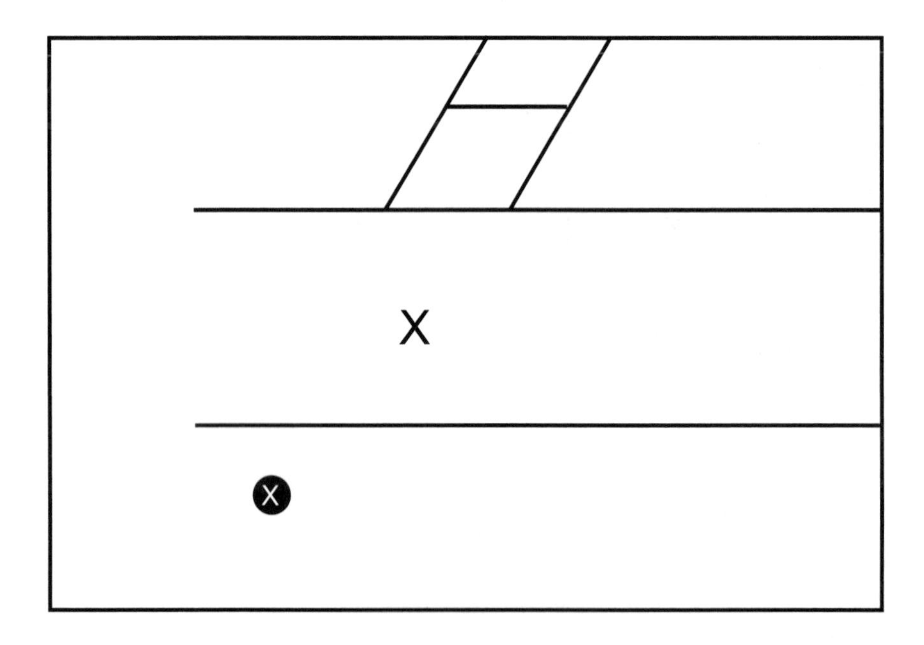

INSTRUCTIONS:

- A player kicks a high ball to a waiting fullback.
- The fullback fields the ball and kicks into touch in an attempt to hit a grid target just outside the touch line.

VARIATIONS:

- A defender may be added to apply pressure.
- Supporting players may be added.
- The fullback may be positioned so that the player must run a rolling ball down and then clear the ball.

38 KICK AND FOLLOW

OBJECTIVE: Improving kicking and catching skills

NUMBER OF PLAYERS: 12

AREA/FIELD: Half field (up to full field)

TIME: 10 minutes

EQUIPMENT: 1 ball, 4 pylons

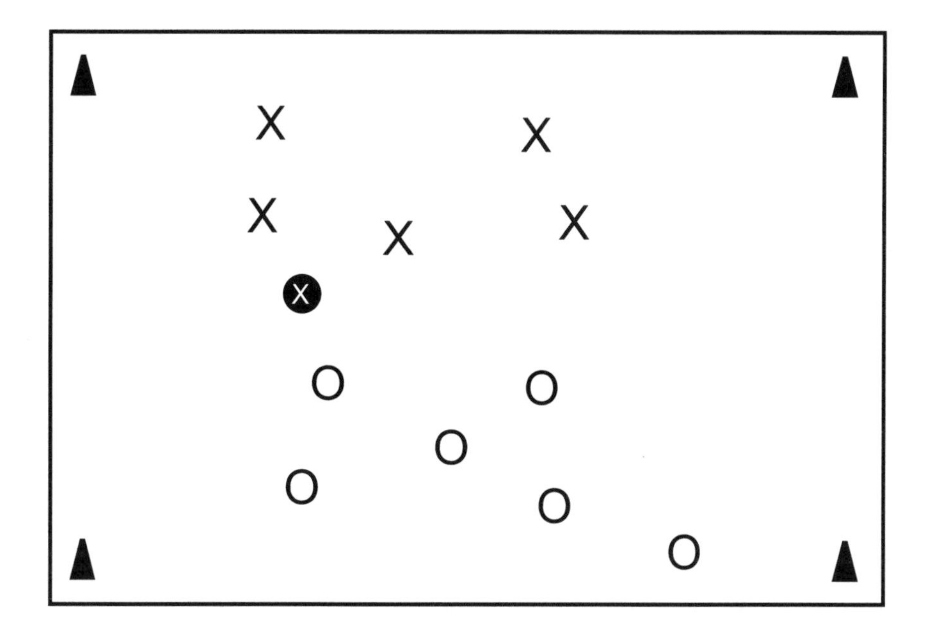

INSTRUCTIONS:

- Organize players into two teams of equal numbers in a narrow grid that runs the length of the field.
- Players attempt to kick the ball so that it lands in the opponent's end zone without their catching it.
- The ball is kicked high in the air and must travel at least 10 meters.
- If the ball is caught before it contacts the ground, the opposition may run the ball back until they are tagged; once tagged, the opposition attempts to kick the ball downfield.
- If the ball hits the ground before being caught, the receiving team may not run the ball back but must kick it from the spot where it hit the ground.

COACHING POINTS:

- Place an emphasis on teaching proper kicking and catching skills.

CONTACT DRILLS

39 HIT AND ROLL

OBJECTIVE: Improving contact skills
NUMBER OF PLAYERS: 12–24
AREA/FIELD: 40 yards × 40 yards
TIME: 10–15 minutes
EQUIPMENT: 4 balls, 4 pylons, 4 blocking pads

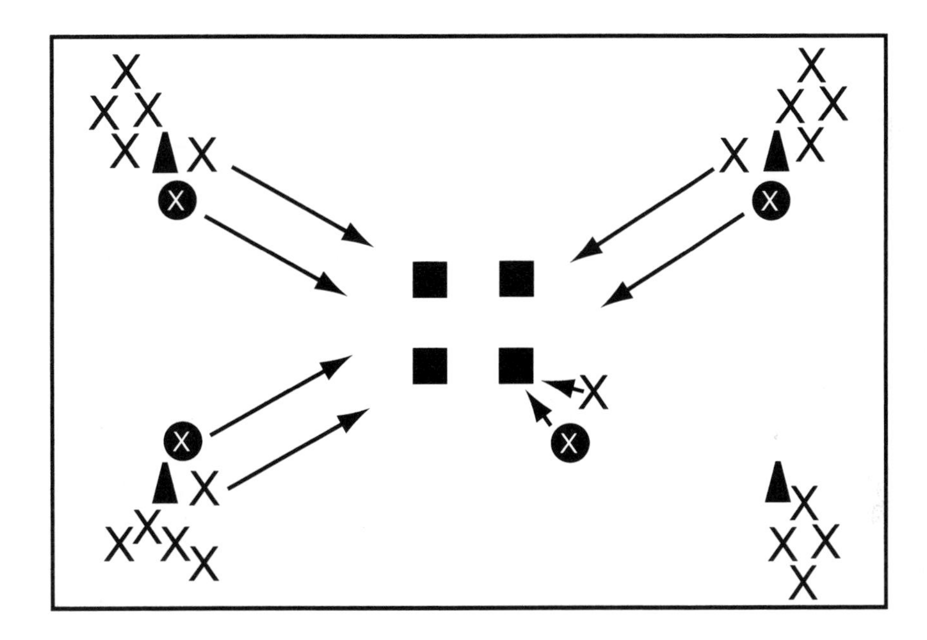

INSTRUCTIONS:

- Organize players in equal groups at each corner of a grid.
- A ball is placed in each corner; four blocking bags are set up in the center of the grid.
- Pairs run across the grid; the ballcarrier hits the pad and the support player rips the ball and rolls away or receives a pass.
- The pair returns to the same corner and hands the ball off to the next group.

COACHING POINTS:

- Contact may be ruck or maul.

VARIATIONS:

- Coach may choose to change the number of players and the mock situation for each attack.

40 WALKING RUGBY

OBJECTIVE: Improving contact and passing skills

NUMBER OF PLAYERS: 12–20

AREA/FIELD: 20 yards × 15 yards

TIME: 10 minutes

EQUIPMENT: 1 ball, 4 pylons

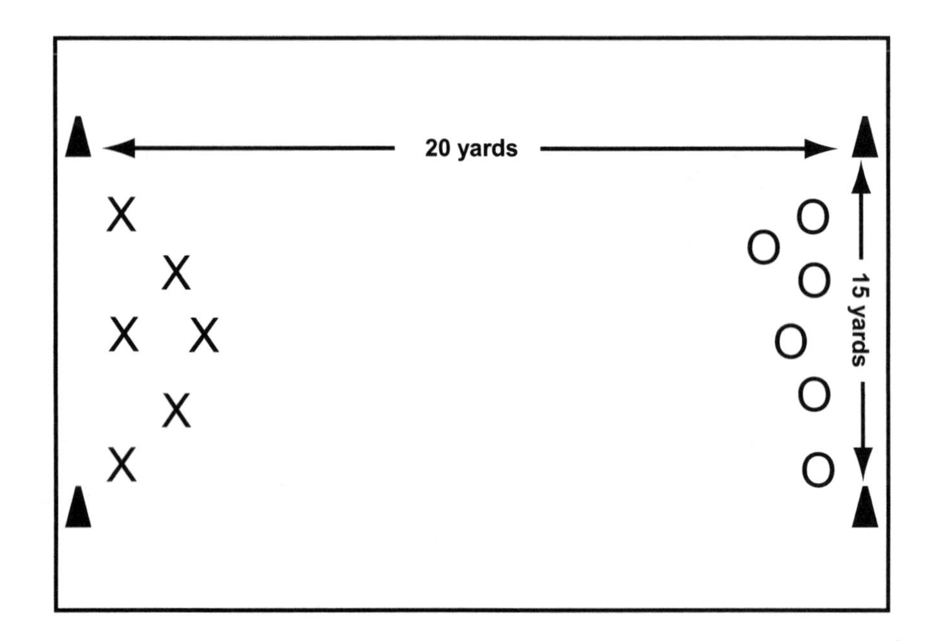

INSTRUCTIONS:

- Organize players into two teams of equal numbers.
- The offensive team attempts to score on the defensive team as in regular rugby.
- Normal rugby rules apply, except all action takes place at a walking pace.

COACHING POINTS:

- When a team goes into contact, it must attempt to come away with the ball and continue the attack.

41 STAY CLOSE

OBJECTIVE: Improving close contact skills
NUMBER OF PLAYERS: 10–14
AREA/FIELD: Half field
TIME: 10 minutes
EQUIPMENT: 1 ball, team pinnies

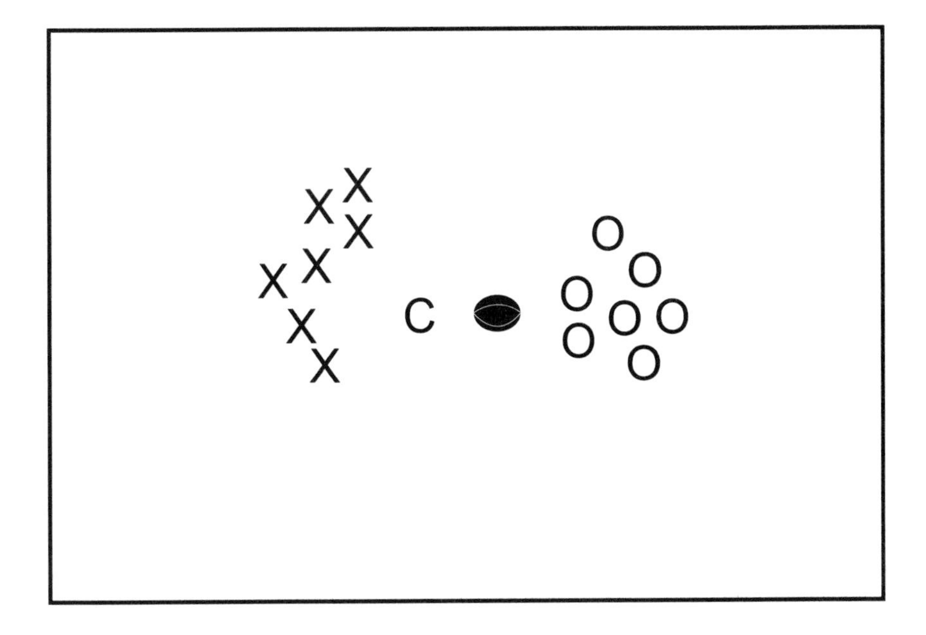

INSTRUCTIONS:

- Teams line up across from each other with a coach in between them.
- The coach has a ball and begins to run; as the coach moves, players from each team (identified by pinnies) must attempt to stay onside.
- When the coach rolls or throws the ball to one side, that team becomes the attacking team and the other team becomes the defense.
- Teams may elect to set up or run the ball.

COACHING POINTS:

- Drill reflects game-like situations.

VARIATIONS:

- Coach may introduce specific counterattack scenarios into play.

42 PARTNER TACKLING

OBJECTIVE: Improving running into contact and support play
NUMBER OF PLAYERS: Pairs (unlimited)
AREA/FIELD: 25 yards × 25 yards
TIME: 8 minutes
EQUIPMENT: 1 ball (per pair)

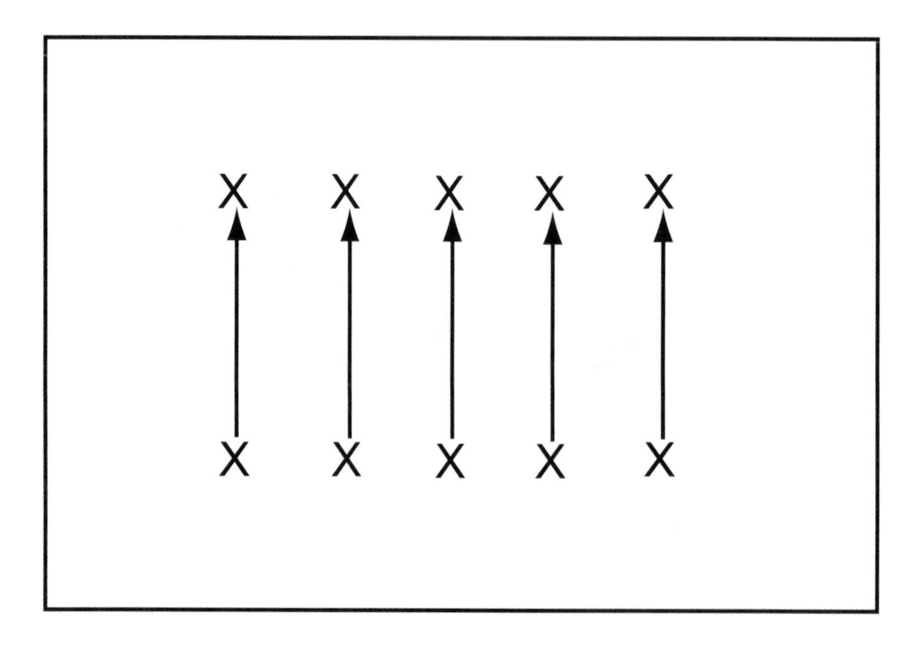

INSTRUCTIONS:

- Organize players in pairs, opposite one another.
- Players practice tackling in progression: first kneeling, then on a knee, then crouching, then standing.
- Players should increase speed of movement from stationary to running and change angle of tackle from head-on to side tackle from behind.
- Players should tackle using both sides of the body.
- Players should practice good tackling technique: head to side, shoulder into thigh, wrap, drive.

COACHING POINTS:

- Drill works great as a warm-up activity.

43 TEAM CHALLENGE

OBJECTIVE: Improving tackling skill and support play

NUMBER OF PLAYERS: 6–20

AREA/FIELD: 30 yards × 30 yards

TIME: 10–15 minutes

EQUIPMENT: 1 ball, 4 pylons

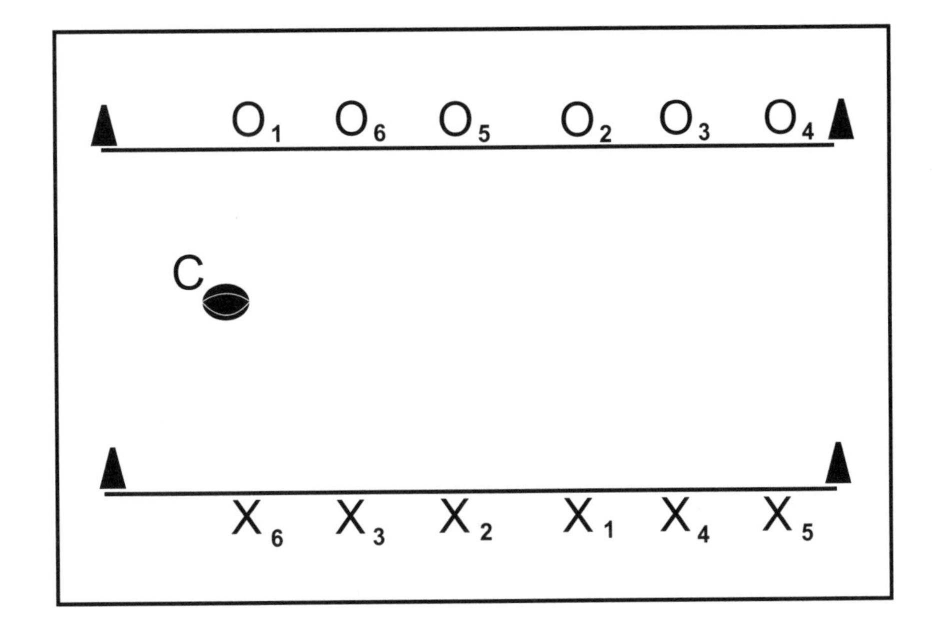

INSTRUCTIONS:

- Organize players into two teams of equal numbers.
- Teams line up on opposite sides of a grid; players on each team spread out in a single-file line.
- Each team assigns its players a number.
- A coach stands between the two teams and calls out the number of one or more players, then passes the ball to one side or the other.
- The player(s) attempt(s) to score across the opposition line.

44 SCORE THE TRY

OBJECTIVE: Improving tackling skill
NUMBER OF PLAYERS: Pairs (unlimited)
AREA/FIELD: 20 yards × 20 yards
TIME: 8 minutes
EQUIPMENT: 1 ball (per pair)

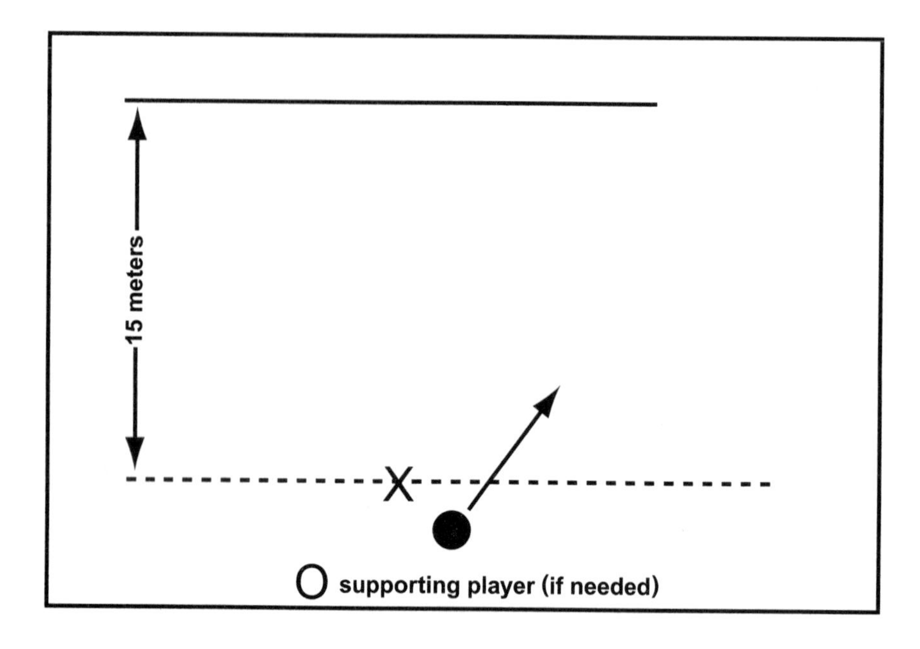

INSTRUCTIONS:
- A tackler lines up 15 meters out from the goal line.
- A runner lines up an additional 5 meters out from the tackler and attempts to score past him.

COACHING POINTS:
- Stress body position and decking the ball after the tackle.

VARIATIONS:
- A runner may attempt to beat additional tacklers; when a runner is stopped, another runner can immediately be substituted into the attack.

45 WHO GETS IT

OBJECTIVE: Improving tackling and passing skills

NUMBER OF PLAYERS: 4

AREA/FIELD: 20 yards × 20 yards

TIME: 6 minutes

EQUIPMENT: 1 ball, 4 pylons

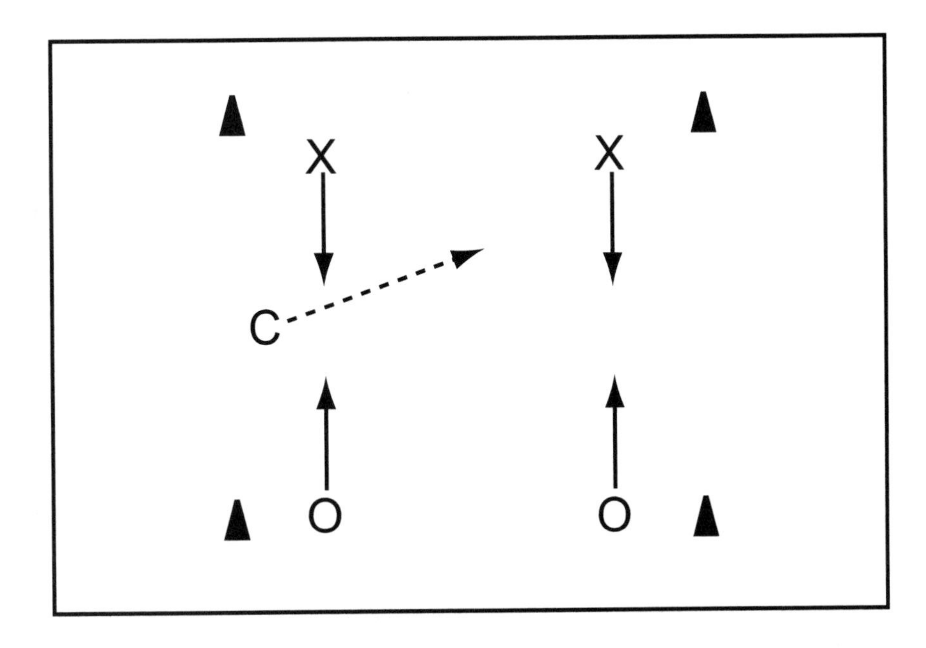

INSTRUCTIONS:

- Two attackers line up against two defenders in a grid area.
- A coach stands between the two attackers and feeds the ball to either one.
- Attackers attempt to score over the grid line behind the defenders.

VARIATIONS:

- Drill may be extended to include support play.

46 2 ON 1

OBJECTIVE: Improving tackling and passing skills

NUMBER OF PLAYERS: 4–20

AREA/FIELD: 40 yards × 40 yards

TIME: 10–15 minutes

EQUIPMENT: 1 ball

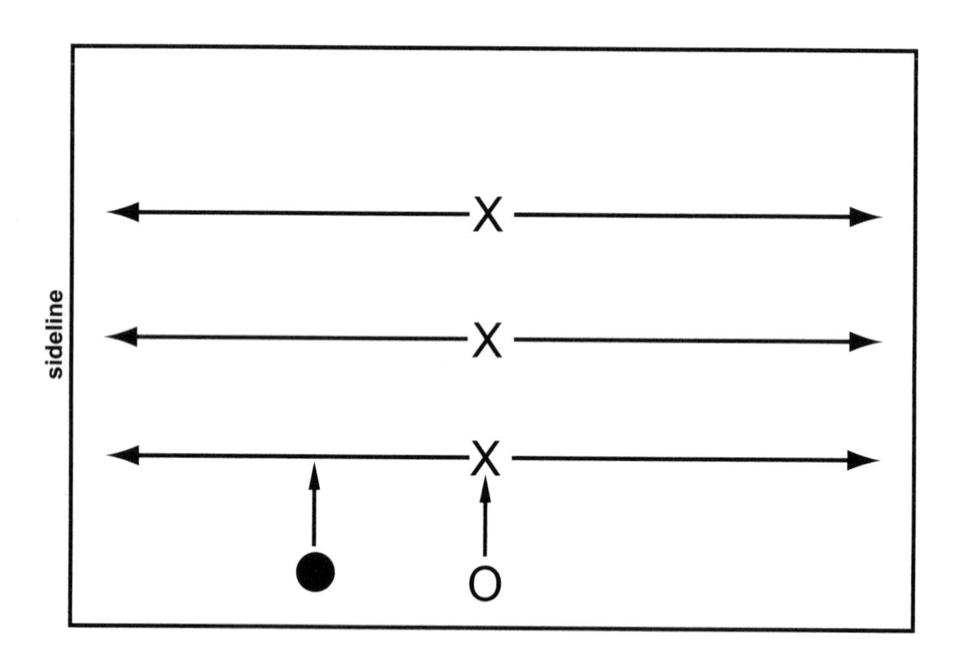

INSTRUCTIONS:

- A pair of attacking players line up facing a series of defenders arranged in chutes.
- Each defender lines up in a separate chute and tries to tackle the attacking player in possession of the ball; defenders are restricted to lateral movement.
- The attacking players attempt to score by running through each defender's chute.

COACHING POINTS:

- It is vital that players run straight and force the opposition to commit.

VARIATIONS:

- Drill may include additional defenders or attackers.
- Drill may use two-hand-touch rules instead of tackle.

47 3-LINE TACKLE

OBJECTIVE: Improving tackling and support skills

NUMBER OF PLAYERS: 6

AREA/FIELD: 20 yards × 20 yards

TIME: 8–10 minutes

EQUIPMENT: 1 ball

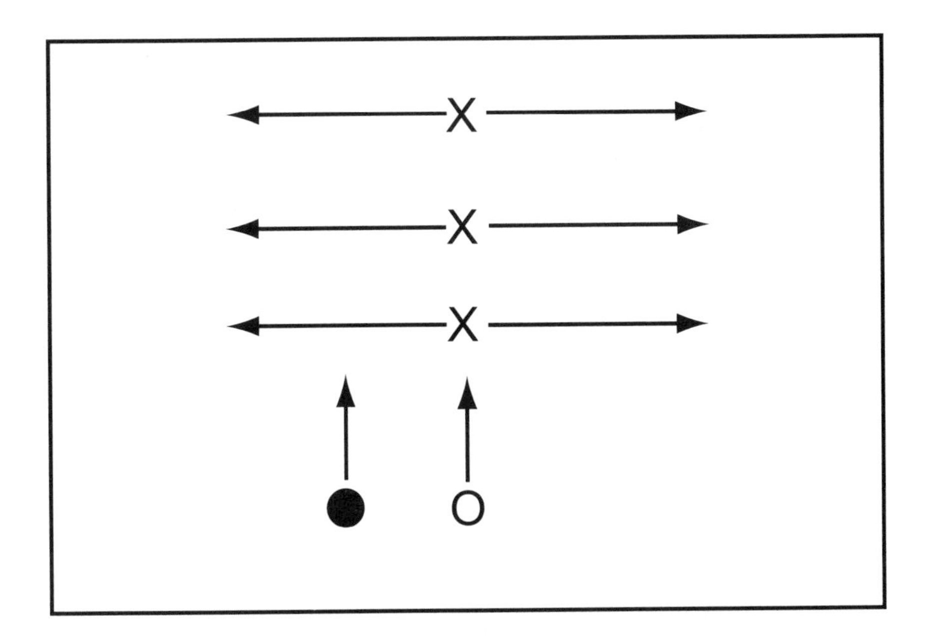

INSTRUCTIONS:

- A pair of attacking players line up facing a series of single defenders arranged in chutes.
- Each defender lines up in a separate chute and tackles the attacking player in possession of the ball; defenders are restricted to lateral movement.
- The supporting player receives the ball from the player being tackled.

COACHING POINTS:

- Players may elect to pass while being tackled or deck the ball.
- A tackled player must get up quickly and continue to support the run.

48 FIRST THERE

OBJECTIVE: Improving open-field play
NUMBER OF PLAYERS: 2–4
AREA/FIELD: 15 yards × 15 yards
TIME: 8 minutes
EQUIPMENT: 1 ball, 4 pylons

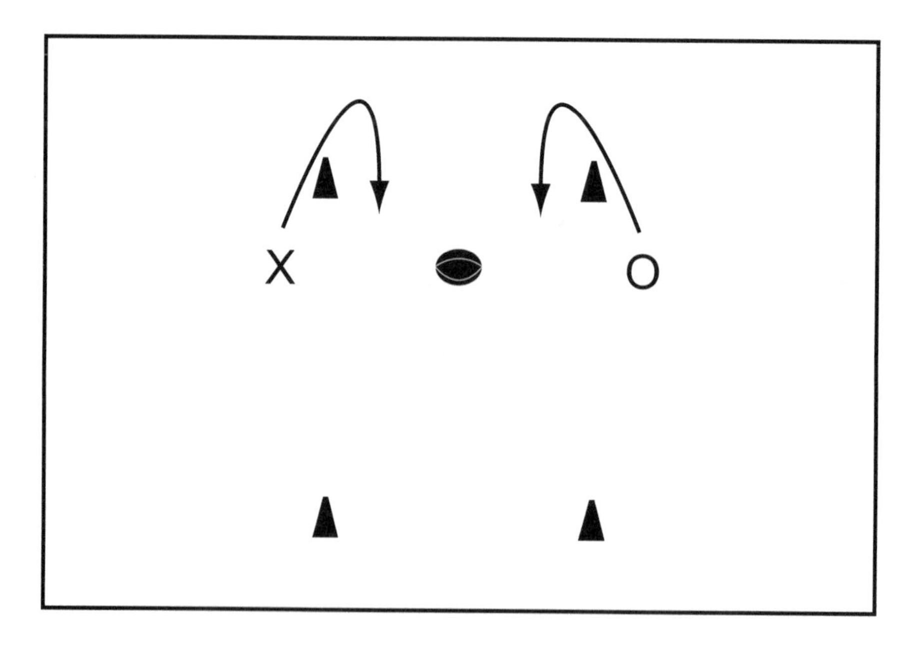

INSTRUCTIONS:

- Two players line up on opposite sides of a square grid area.
- A ball is placed on the ground halfway between the players inside the square.
- Each player races around a pylon in an attempt to reach the ball first.
- The first player to the ball attempts to score by running through the pylons at the other end of the square.
- The other player becomes a tackler and tries to keep the runner from scoring.

COACHING POINTS:

- Clarify rugby laws regarding open-field play.

VARIATIONS:

- Drill can also be carried out in pairs.

49 PURSUIT DRILL

OBJECTIVE: Improving ballhandling skills and pursuit lines

NUMBER OF PLAYERS: 12–16

AREA/FIELD: Half field

TIME: 10–15 minutes

EQUIPMENT: 4 balls

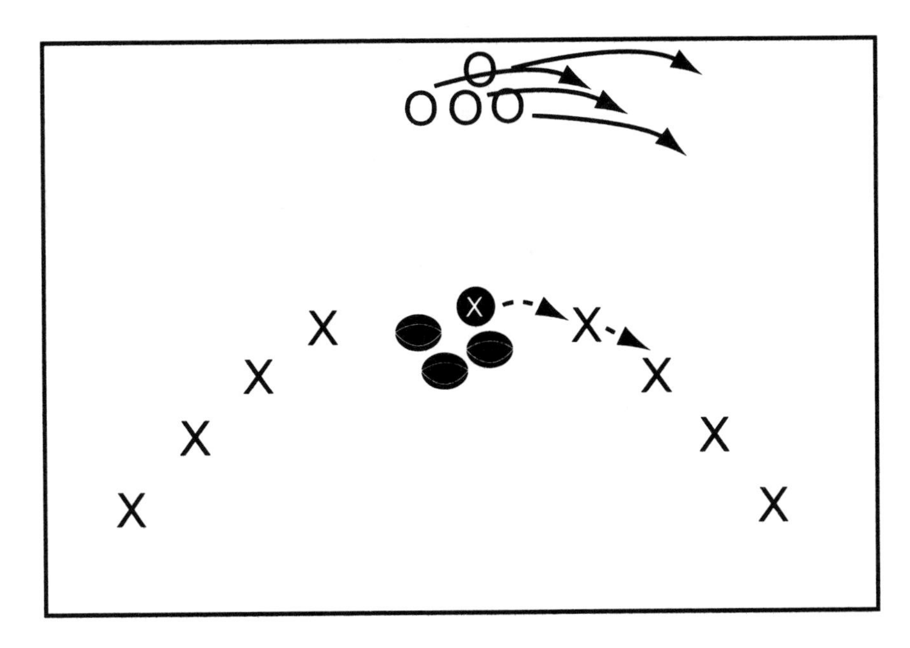

INSTRUCTIONS:

- Set up the scrum half (with four balls) in the middle of the field; place a back line to either side and position a group of defenders 5 meters in front.
- When the scrum half feeds a ball to a back line, defenders chase the ball out in that direction.
- On the coach's command, the scrum half feeds the other back line and the defenders chase the second set of attackers in the other direction.
- The scrum half should feed the balls on alternating sides.

COACHING POINTS:

- Back-line players should work on ballhandling, realignment, and fitness.
- Defenders should work on pursuit lines and fitness.

50 4-TEAM CHALLENGE

OBJECTIVE: Improving passing skills (under pressure)
NUMBER OF PLAYERS: 12–16
AREA/FIELD: 20 yards × 20 yards
TIME: 10–15 minutes
EQUIPMENT: 4 balls, 4 pylons

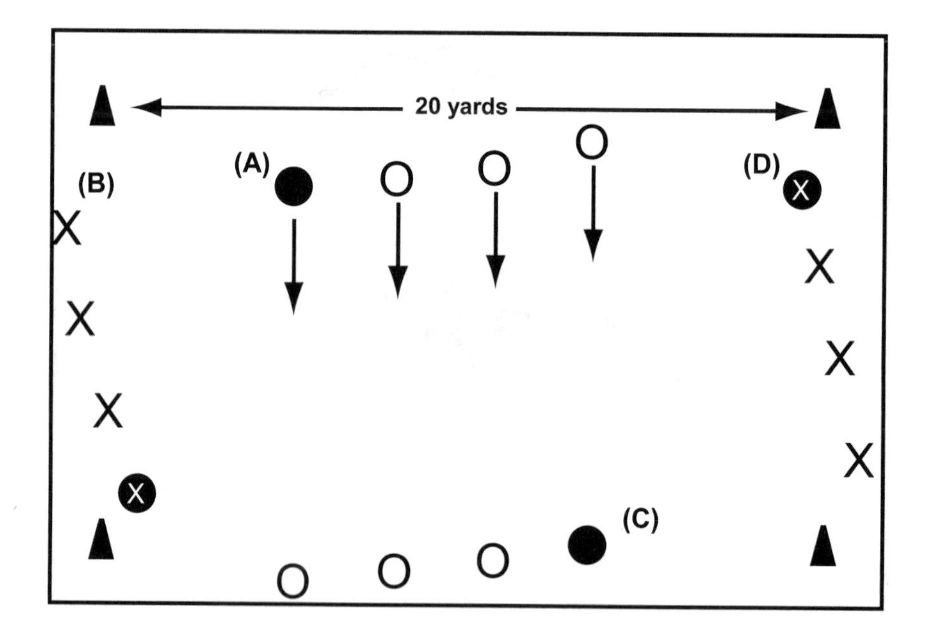

INSTRUCTIONS:

- Organize players into groups of equal numbers in a grid area.
- A letter is assigned to each group.
- When the coach calls out a signal, the appropriate group crosses the grid to the opposite side.
- The ball begins on the far right of each group.

COACHING POINTS:

- Drill forces players to keep their heads up.

VARIATIONS:

- Coach may call out multiple groups at the same time; groups may choose to have a player loop or switch.

51 BUILD IT (MAUL AND RUCK)

OBJECTIVE: Improving rucking and mauling skills
NUMBER OF PLAYERS: 10–12
AREA/FIELD: Half field
TIME: 10–15 minutes
EQUIPMENT: 1 ball (per group), 4 blocking pads

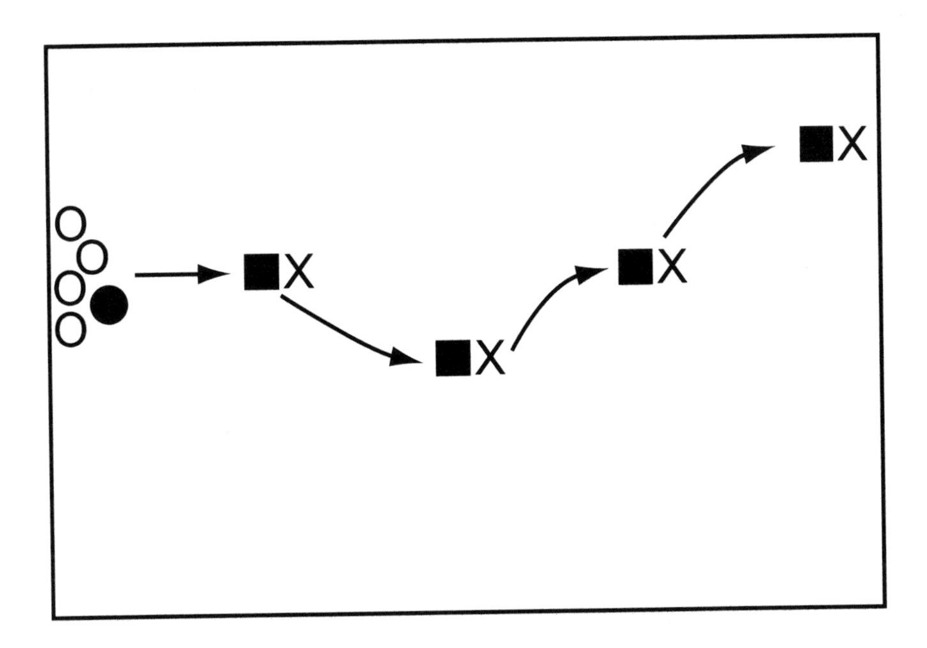

INSTRUCTIONS:

- A group of attacking players faces a zigzag formation of opposition points up the field.
- The attacking group attempts to advance the ball up the field through the line of defense.
- Defenders may challenge the attacking team's advance with token defense (simply holding blocking pads) or full opposition (contact).
- The attacking group moves from one point of contact to the next.
- Coaches will make decisions regarding the intensity and number of the opposition.

COACHING POINTS: Drill is excellent for working on player fitness.

VARIATIONS:

- Coach may elect to go straight into the ruck, maul, or tackle.
- Coach may incorporate a progression of skills into the drill, such as:

a) Group may enter contact situation, working on presenting the ball for either a ruck, maul, or tackle.

b) Group may work on support play, with the first player to a maul securing possession.

c) Group may start with two in and slowly add more players, with the supporting players simply trailing the play.

d) Group may work on player speed by adding a scrum half, and increasing the speed of the ball, etc.

52 LINE RUCK OR MAUL

OBJECTIVE: Improving rucking and mauling skills

NUMBER OF PLAYERS: 8–12

AREA/FIELD: 25 yards × 25 yards

TIME: 10 minutes

EQUIPMENT: 1 ball

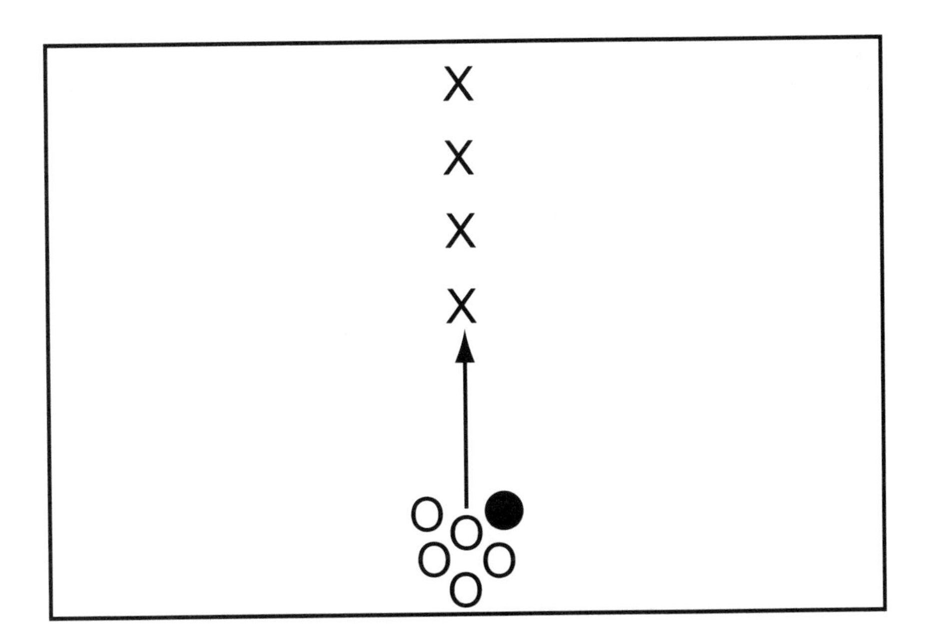

INSTRUCTIONS:

- A group of attackers faces a line of defenders.
- The attackers run the ball directly at the defenders.
- Defenders can be token or fully opposed.

COACHING POINTS:

- Attackers should outnumber defenders and should therefore win the ball.
- Coach may designate that all mauls are sets, rucks, or combinations.

53 CONTINUOUS RUGBY

OBJECTIVE: Improving team play
NUMBER OF PLAYERS: 12–16
AREA/FIELD: Half field
TIME: 10–15 minutes
EQUIPMENT: 1 ball, 4 pylons

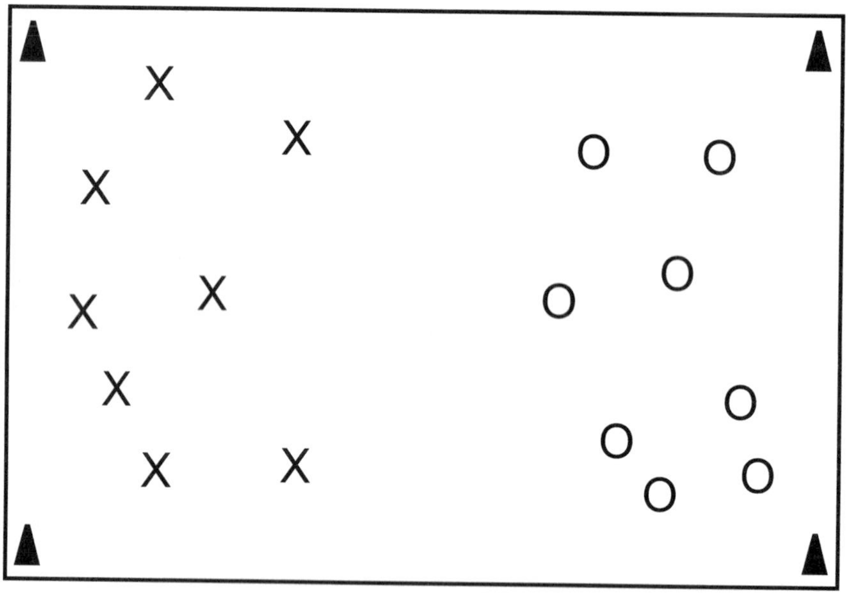

INSTRUCTIONS:

- Organize two teams in a grid area.
- Attacking players attempt to score by getting the ball over the opposition goal line; attackers can pass the ball in any direction.
- Defenders attempt to tag attackers in possession of the ball.
- A tagged player cannot run with the ball but must pass it (opposition coverage is similar to that of basketball).
- A dropped ball results in a turnover.
- Normal rugby rules, except players must walk.
- Drill may be run with full contact.

RUNNING DRILLS

54 SHADOW

OBJECTIVE: Improving running skills
NUMBER OF PLAYERS: 2
AREA/FIELD: Half field
TIME: 4 minutes
EQUIPMENT: 1 ball (per pair)

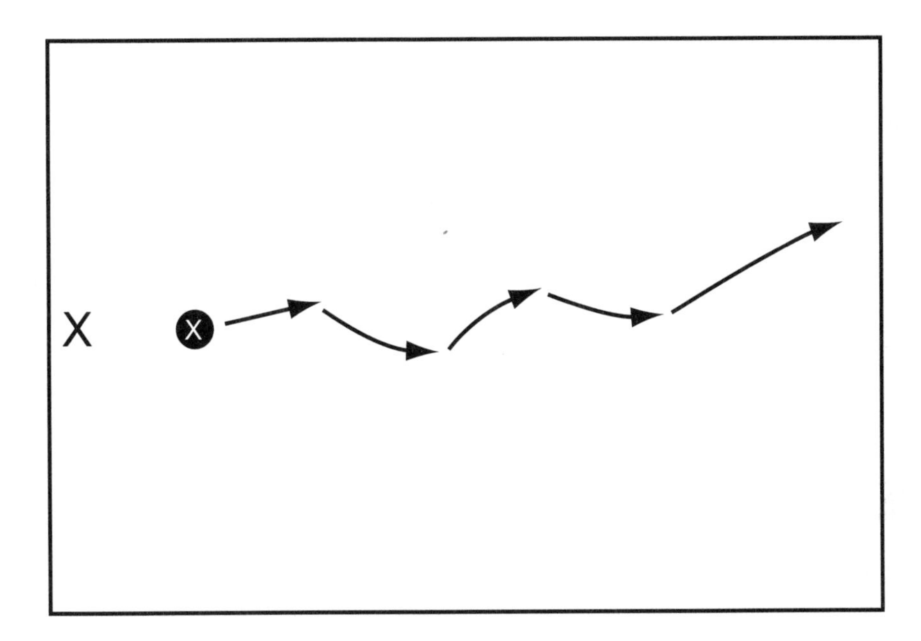

INSTRUCTIONS:

- A runner stands an arm's length behind a partner.
- The front runner changes speeds and directions in an attempt to increase the distance between the two.
- The back player tries to shadow the front runner and maintain the token distance (or keep it as close as possible).
- Players alternate roles.

55 TURN AND RUN

OBJECTIVE: Improving running skills
NUMBER OF PLAYERS: 2
AREA/FIELD: 10 yards × 10 yards
TIME: 4 minutes
EQUIPMENT: 1 ball, 1 pylon

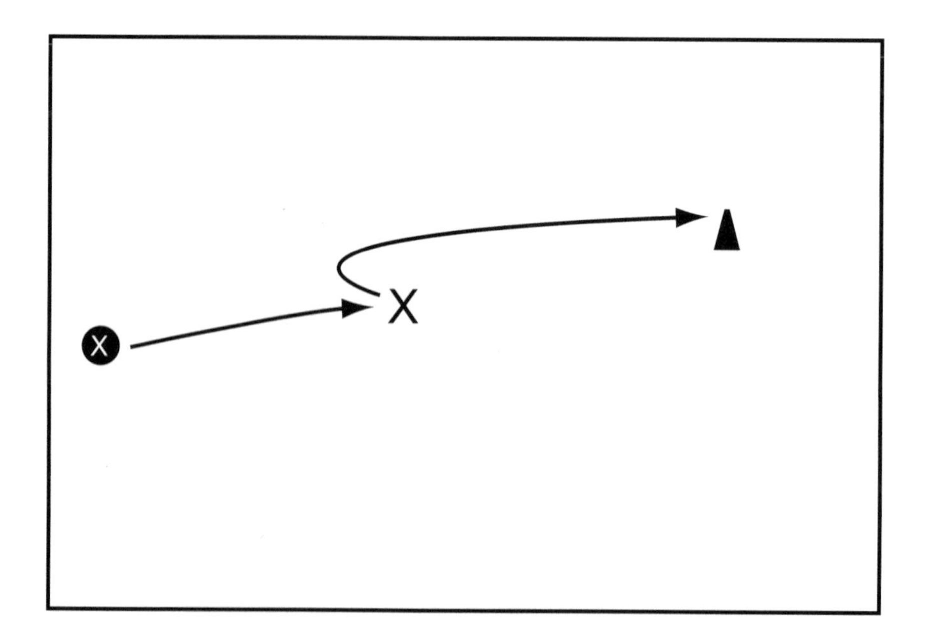

INSTRUCTIONS:

- A runner stands 2 meters away from a defender (distance may vary according to player ability).
- The defender yells "run" and the runner attempts to carry the ball past a pylon before being tagged.
- Players alternate roles.

56 BULLRUSH

OBJECTIVE: Improving running skills
NUMBER OF PLAYERS: 2
AREA/FIELD: 20 yards × 20 yards
TIME: 8 minutes
EQUIPMENT: 1 ball, 4 pylons

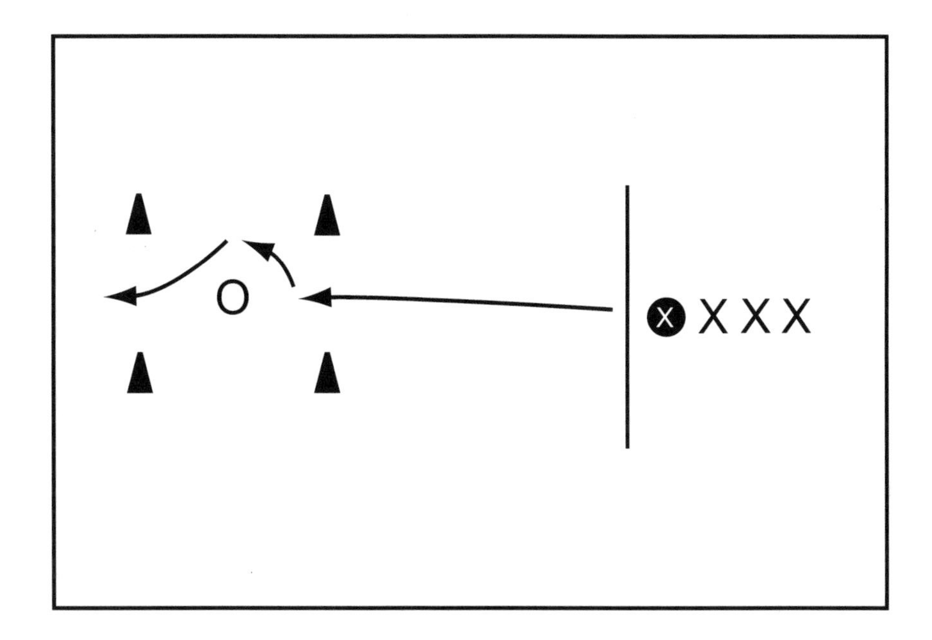

INSTRUCTIONS:

- Runners form a line in front of an area marked off by pylons; a single player is positioned inside the pylons and guards the area between them.
- The guard can only move sideways within the marked area and must stay within the pylons.
- Runners carry a ball one at a time into the guarded area and attempt to make it past the guard; runners use feints, change of pace, change of direction, etc. to try to fool the guard.
- Players alternate roles.

57 PAIRS TAG

OBJECTIVE: Improving running skills
NUMBER OF PLAYERS: 12–14
AREA/FIELD: 20 yards × 20 yards
TIME: 8 minutes
EQUIPMENT: 4 pylons

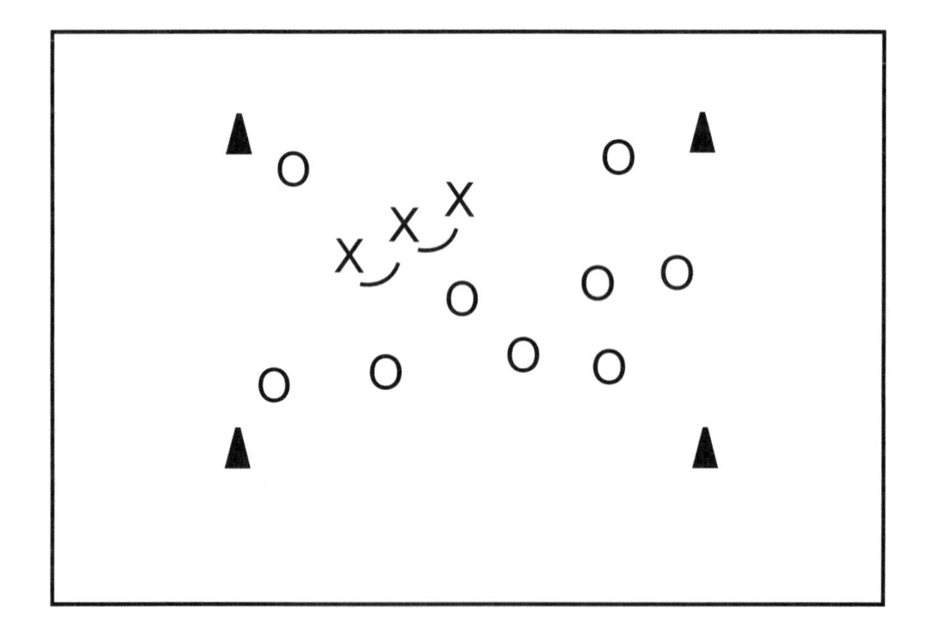

INSTRUCTIONS:

- Players move freely about a given area—a pair is designated to be taggers; all others are runners.
- The pair join hands and move around in an attempt to tag runners.
- When a runner is tagged, that player must join hands with the group.
- Once a group reaches four taggers, it must split into two pairs.
- Each group continues in an attempt to tag additional runners, splitting into pairs anytime a group of four is formed.
- Repeat the process until all runners are tagged.

COACHING POINTS:

- Drill provides an effective warm-up activity.

58 STUCK IN THE MUD

OBJECTIVE: Improving running skills

NUMBER OF PLAYERS: 10–20

AREA/FIELD: 25 yards × 25 yards

TIME: 8 minutes

EQUIPMENT: 4 pylons

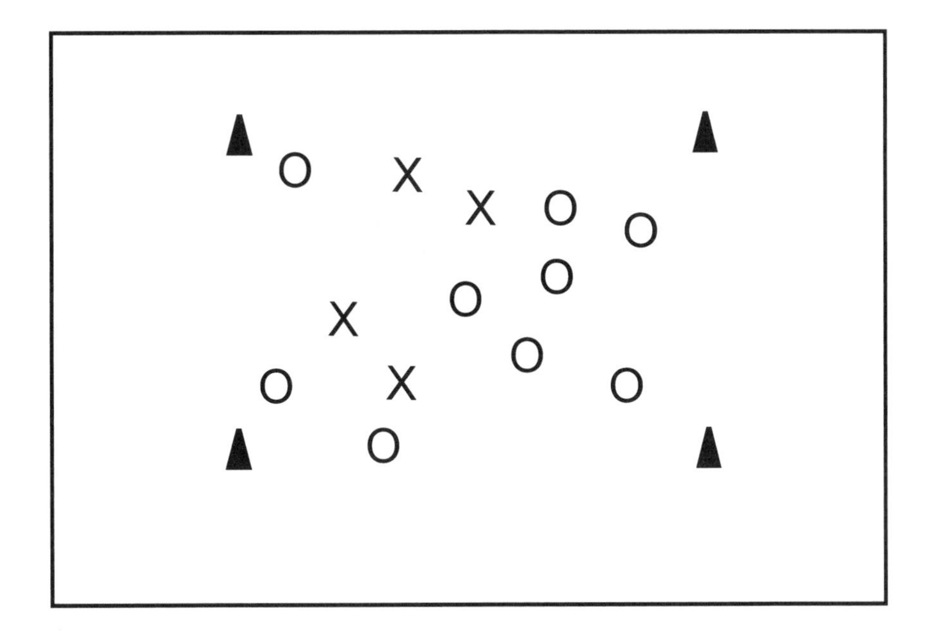

INSTRUCTIONS:

- Players move freely about a given area—a group is designated to be taggers; all others are runners.
- Taggers attempt to tag as many runners as possible in a given amount of time (i.e., 2 minutes)
- When a runner is tagged, that player must immediately freeze (leaving both his feet apart).
- In order for a frozen player to rejoin the game, an unfrozen teammate must crawl through his legs.
- Each group tallies the number of frozen players at the end of the time (2 minutes).
- Players alternate roles; a new group of runners become taggers and attempt to tally more frozen players than previous groups.

COACHING POINTS:

- Drill provides an effective warm-up for younger players.

59 BUMP

OBJECTIVE: Improving running and dodging skills

NUMBER OF PLAYERS: 11–20

AREA/FIELD: 30 yards × 30 yards

TIME: 8 minutes

EQUIPMENT: 4 pylons

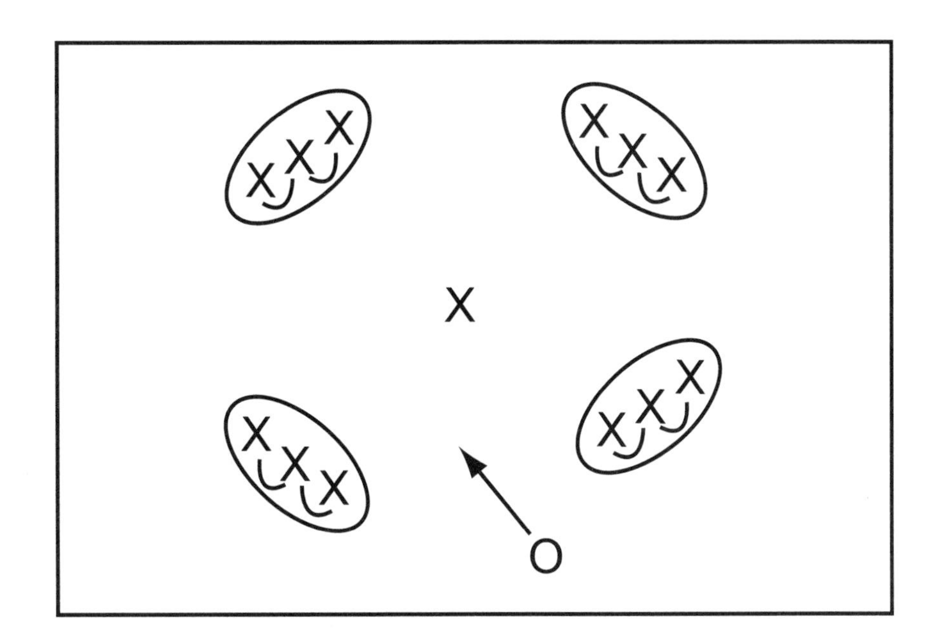

INSTRUCTIONS:

- A runner and a tagger move freely about a given area; all other players link arms in stationary groups of three.
- The runner attempts to avoid the tagger.
- The runner may join onto a group to avoid being tagged by linking arms with the group.
- When a runner joins onto a group, the player at the opposite end of the group is bumped off and becomes the new runner.
- When a runner is tagged, that player becomes the new tagger; the former tagger becomes the new runner.

COACHING POINTS:

- Drill provides a simple and effective warm-up.

60 OCTOPUS

OBJECTIVE: Improving running and dodging skills

NUMBER OF PLAYERS: 20–30

AREA/FIELD: 25 yards × 25 yards

TIME: 8 minutes

EQUIPMENT: 4 pylons

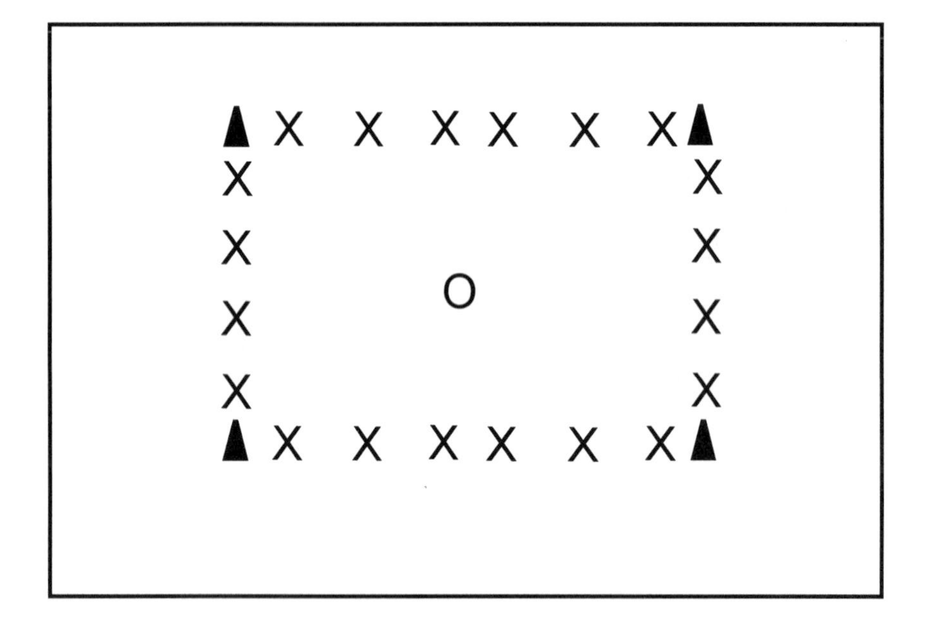

INSTRUCTIONS:

- Place a single player (octopus) inside a square marked by pylons and position all other players along the outside boundaries of the square (dimensions dependent on the number and ability of players).
- On a call from the octopus, all players must cross to the opposite side of the square, dodging the octopus as they move.
- The octopus attempts to tag moving players.
- A player must stop immediately when tagged.
- A tagged player becomes a tentacle; tentacles cannot move around but can use their arms to tag other players trying to run through.
- The last person through becomes the new octopus.

61 EVASION

OBJECTIVE: Improving running and tackling skills
NUMBER OF PLAYERS: 5–10
AREA/FIELD: 20 yards × 20 yards
TIME: 10 minutes
EQUIPMENT: 1 ball, 12 pylons

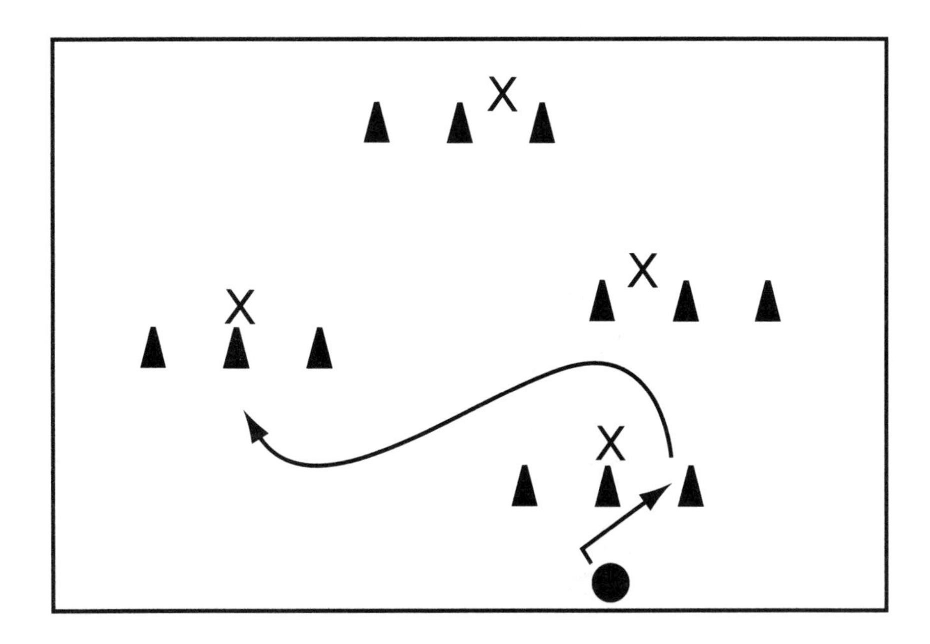

INSTRUCTIONS:

- Position cones as makeshift gates for ballcarrying runners to maneuver through.
- A tackler is placed between the cones.
- A runner challenges the tackler head to head and chooses to run left or right.

COACHING POINTS:

- Additional runners and attackers may be added to the drill.

62 FEND OFF

OBJECTIVE: Improving fend-off skills
NUMBER OF PLAYERS: 6–10
AREA/FIELD: 20 yards × 20 yards
TIME: 8–10 minutes
EQUIPMENT: 1 ball

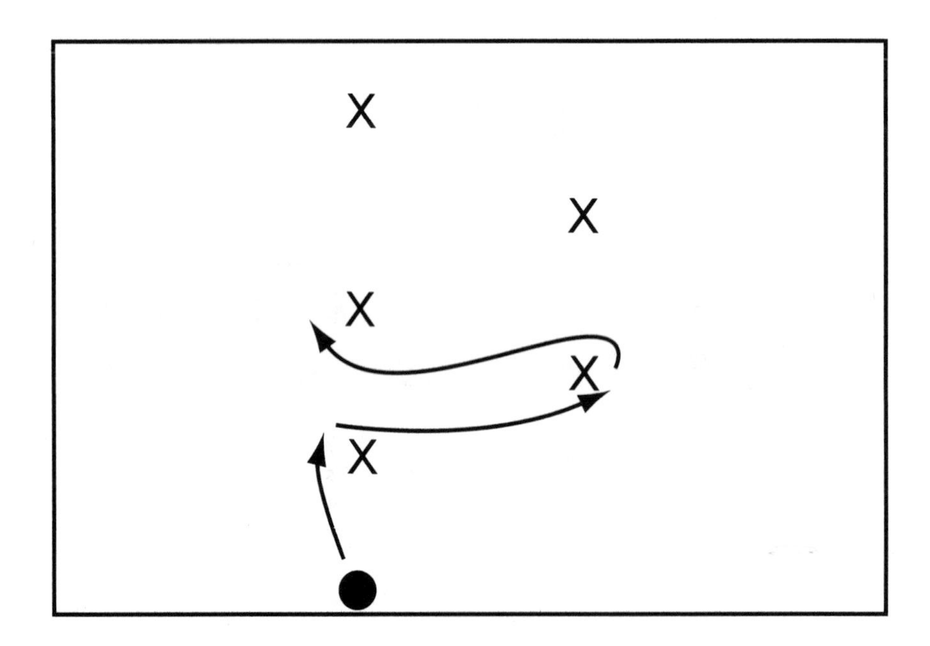

INSTRUCTIONS:
- A runner carrying a ball runs through a maze of kneeling players acting as token defenders.
- The runner must fend off the kneeling players.

COACHING POINTS:
- Players should try to maintain a lower center of gravity and swing the hips away from tacklers.

5

BACK PLAY

POINTS TO CONSIDER

This chapter provides coaches with a variety of plays used by the back line. It is important to remember to run a few plays well, rather than run several plays poorly. To make the diagrams easy to follow and understand, I have numbered the participating players as listed below:

PLAYER KEY

1 – Scrum Half

2 – Fly Half

3 – Inside Center

4 – Outside Center

5 – Wingers (blindside winger also)

6 – Fullback

The back line must be agile and possess excellent open-field tackling capabilities. Forwards are primarily the ball winners. The essential function of backs is to score tries, but backs are also responsible for coming up in defense to prevent the opposition from scoring.

To put it simply, the rugby back is a position under constant pressure. Pressure comes courtesy of the opposition backs and forwards. Another element of pressure comes from the fact that rugby backs are required to execute skills at high speeds while maintaining continuity. As a result, it is often quite obvious when a back makes an error. The consequence in such a situation can be disastrous. Mistakes made by forwards, on the other hand, are generally recoverable. Either way, the key is to develop continuity in the back line.

It is a good idea to start off slowly and add further plays as your back line gains confidence. Remember, it is completely acceptable to take any of the plays described and change or modify them to fit the needs of your players and team. The key is to pass well and to pass quickly. None of the plays will prove successful if ball movement is slow or if the ball is dropped.

Your team's effectiveness is dependent on its ability to function as a coordinated group. Regardless of the talent and skill of your back line, success will come as a result of combined effort.

POSITIONAL REQUIREMENTS

Each back-line position has its own unique characteristics. With experience, a player better understands how to develop those characteristics.

SCRUM HALF

The following are the positional requirements of the scrum half:

- excellent passing skills, ability to pass quickly and accurately
- ability to kick in defense and attack
- ability to defend against back-row moves
- ideally, a player who is left-handed and right-footed, since this player follows the ball from left to right in the scrum (the left-hand, right-foot orientation serves to protect the ball when passing)

FLY HALF

The following are the positional requirements of the fly half:

- responsible for initiating team attack
- responsible for organizing and ensuring that centers are up on defense
- ability to handle and catch the ball cleanly and consistently
- ability to kick on attack and defense
- ability to handle the ball while running or while standing still

CENTER

The following are the positional requirements of the center:

- ability to pass quickly and accurately
- ability to tackle effectively
- ability to handle the ball well in contact
- ability to find the gap

WINGER

The following are the positional requirements of the winger:

- demonstrated speed
- excellent defensive skills (this is an area that the opposition often attacks)
- ability to counterattack deep kicks
- ability to cover the fullback position when on the blind side of the field

FULLBACK

The following are the positional requirements of the fullback:

- ability to kick accurately and handle the high kick
- ability to enter the back line decisively
- excellent counterattacking skills
- excellent open-field tackling skills (this being the last line of defense)

BASIC BACK ALIGNMENT

A knowledge of basic back alignment is a key to running effective back plays. Although the primary functions of the back position are offensive, there are also defensive considerations to keep in mind. On the following pages I will describe four basic alignments and include diagrams. These plays address attack formation from the lineout and scrum as well as defensive formation from the lineout.

63 ATTACKING FROM THE LINEOUT

OBJECTIVE: Basic positioning
NUMBER OF PLAYERS: 30
AREA/FIELD: Full field

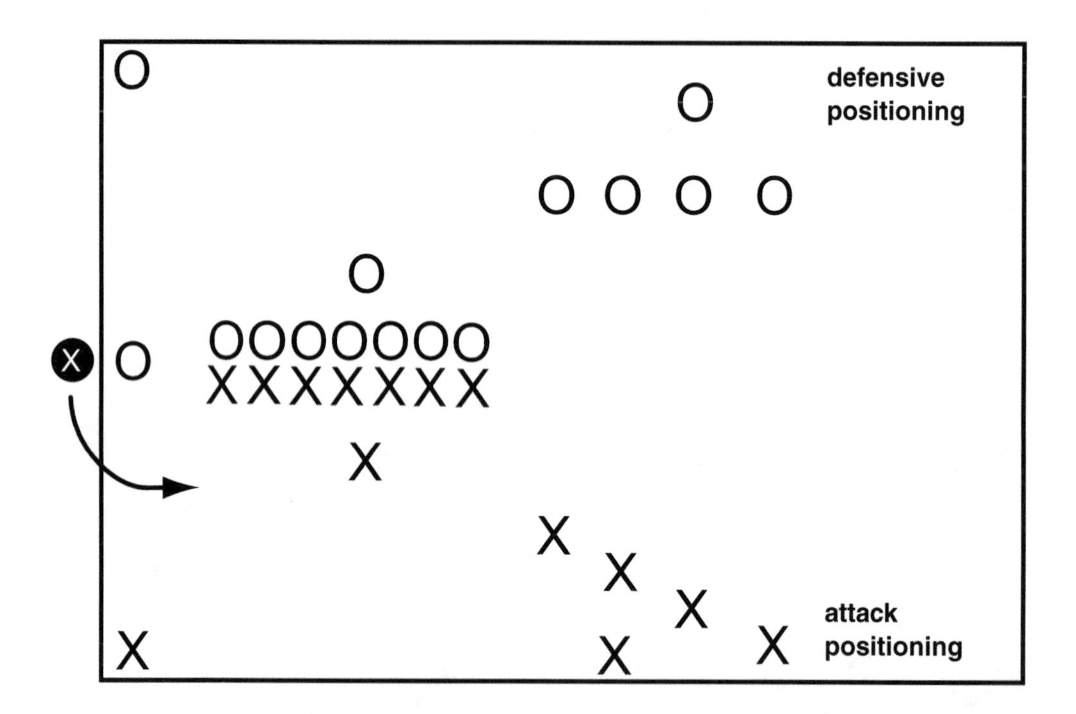

INSTRUCTIONS:

- Alignment is steep in attack to allow backs to run onto the ball.
- The spacing (gap) between the scrum half and the fly half is determined by playing conditions and the passing ability of the scrum half.
- The back line must be at least 10 meters back from the lineout.

COACHING POINTS:

- If the lineout has moved a meter or the ball has been tapped, the backs can move up to the hindmost foot.

64 DEFENDING FROM THE LINEOUT

OBJECTIVE: Basic positioning
NUMBER OF PLAYERS: 30
AREA/FIELD: Full field

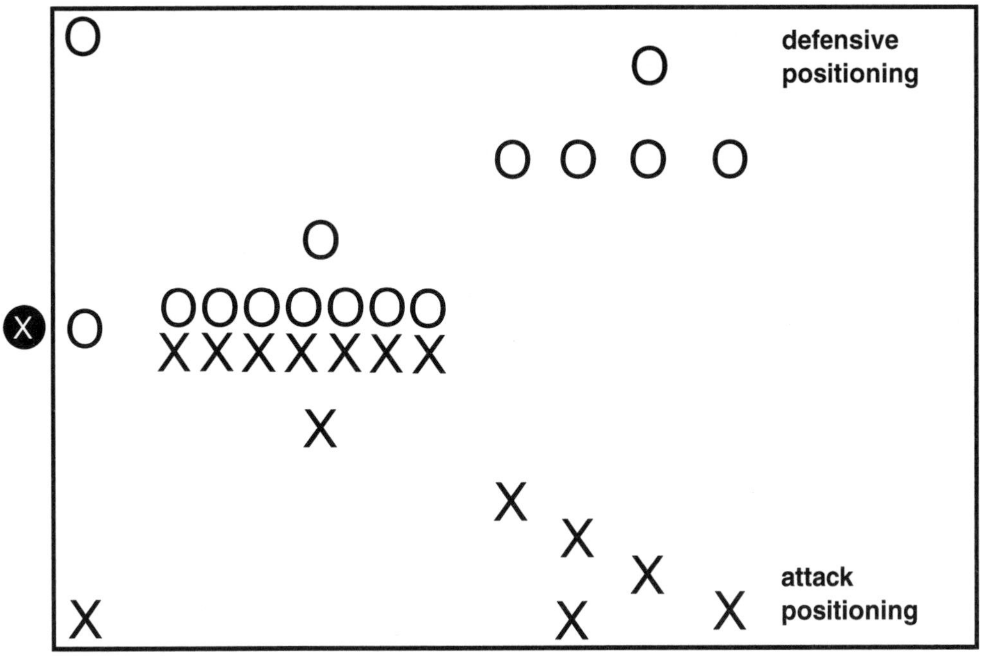

defensive positioning

attack positioning

INSTRUCTIONS:

- The back line should stand 10 meters back from the opposition.
- Players should stand just outside the outside shoulder of the opponent.

COACHING POINTS:

- Players must come up together quickly and always in control; players must also come up together flat so that the opposition has no gaps through which to attack.

65 ATTACKING FROM THE SCRUM

OBJECTIVE: Basic positioning
NUMBER OF PLAYERS: 30
AREA/FIELD: Full field

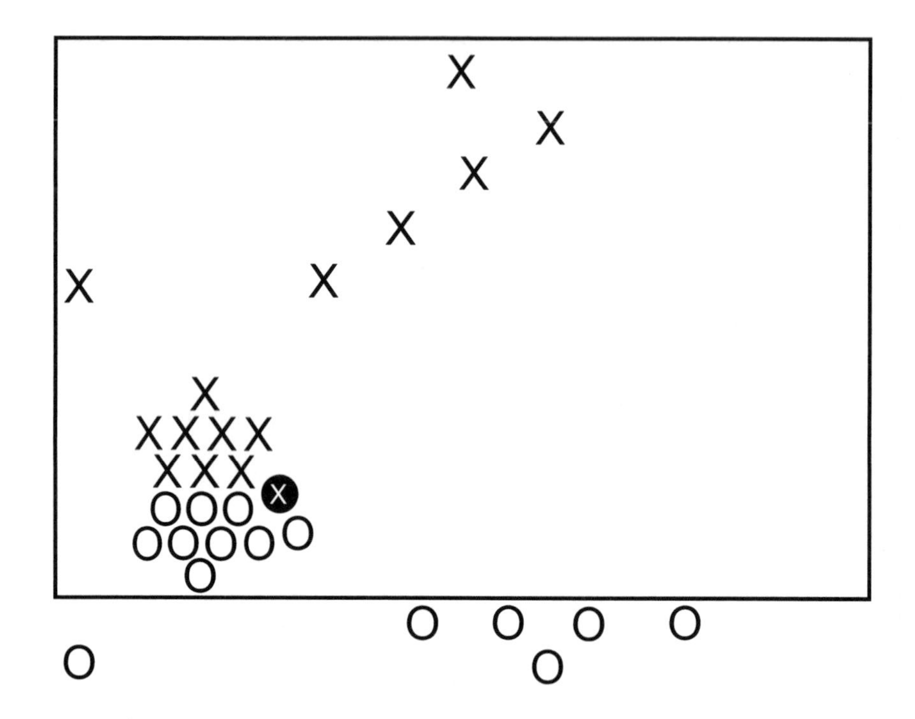

INSTRUCTIONS:
- The distance that backs line up from a scrum is set by the fly half.
- The fly half may elect to align a bit deeper in order to create space for particular back moves.

COACHING POINTS:
- Backs must be at least behind the hindmost foot.

66 DRIFT DEFENSE FROM A LINEOUT

OBJECTIVE: Drift defense
NUMBER OF PLAYERS: 30
AREA/FIELD: Full field

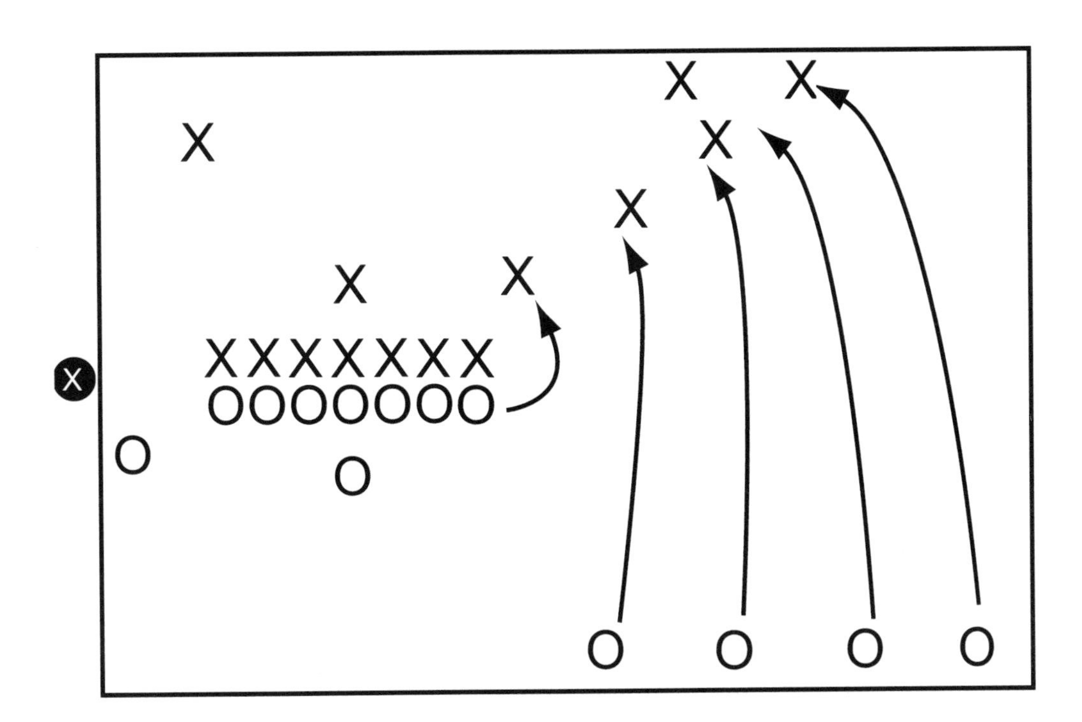

INSTRUCTIONS:

- In this basic defensive system, each player simply defends the player one position over (i.e., fly half becomes responsible for the inside center, etc.).
- This system is generally used only from defense from a lineout.
- This system creates an extra defender.

COACHING POINTS:

- The player at the back of the lineout must cover the fly half.

ASSORTED BACK PLAYS

Back plays are carried out by the scrum half, the fly half, the two centers (inside/ outside), the wingers, and the fullback. Remember the general guideline—learn to run a few plays effectively rather than several plays poorly. On the following pages I will describe an assortment of back plays and include diagrams.

67 STRAIGHT OUT (THROUGH THE HANDS)

OBJECTIVE: Back play
NUMBER OF PLAYERS: 7
AREA/FIELD: Half field (up to full field)
TIME: 7–8 minutes
EQUIPMENT: 1 ball

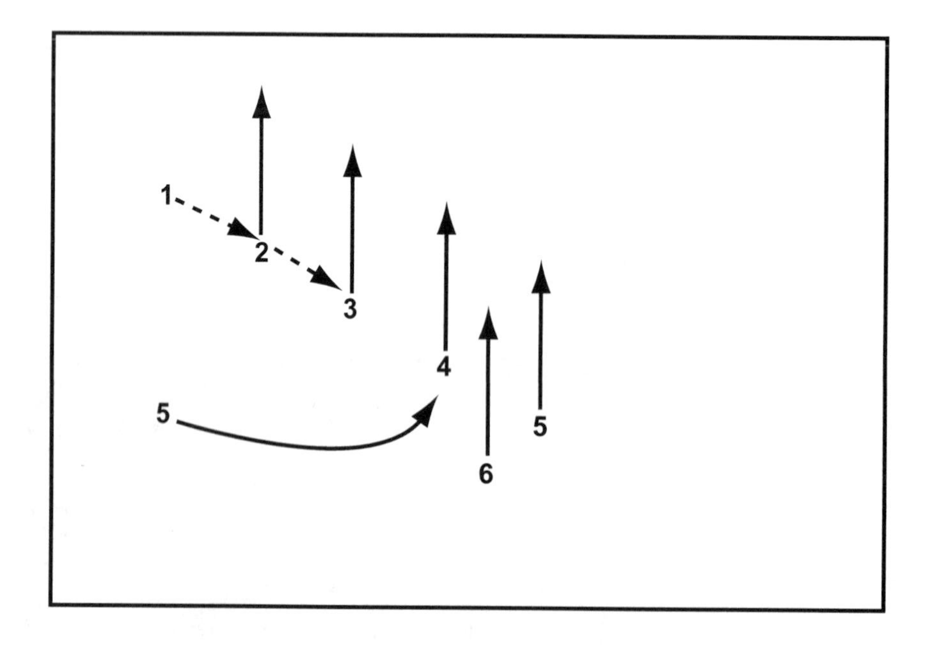

INSTRUCTIONS:

- The ball moves from the scrum half to the fly half and on down the line.
- The fullback should attack on all possessions.
- The blind-side winger covers across for the fullback.

COACHING POINTS:

- This method is by far the most common way to move the ball.
- It is vital that backs learn to move the ball effectively; they must concentrate on moving the ball quickly while keeping it out in front of their bodies.

68 MISS 3

OBJECTIVE: Back play
NUMBER OF PLAYERS: 7
AREA/FIELD: Half field (up to full field)
TIME: 7–8 minutes
EQUIPMENT: 1 ball

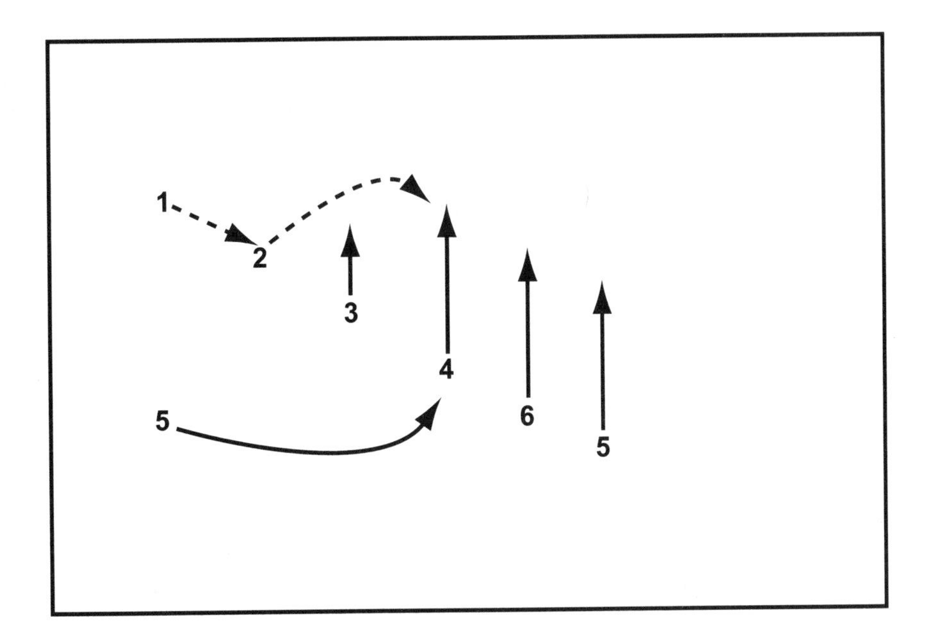

INSTRUCTIONS:

- The scrum half passes the ball to the fly half.
- The fly half misses the inside center position and hits the outside center.
- The outside center crashes into contact or links with the winger and fullback in support.
- The blind-side winger covers for the fullback.

COACHING POINTS:

- After the inside center has been missed, that player should loop to support the play.
- The inside center must wait until the ball has been passed to the outside center before moving to support the play.

69 MISS 4 HIT 6

OBJECTIVE: Back play
NUMBER OF PLAYERS: 7
AREA/FIELD: Half field (up to full field)
TIME: 7–8 minutes
EQUIPMENT: 1 ball

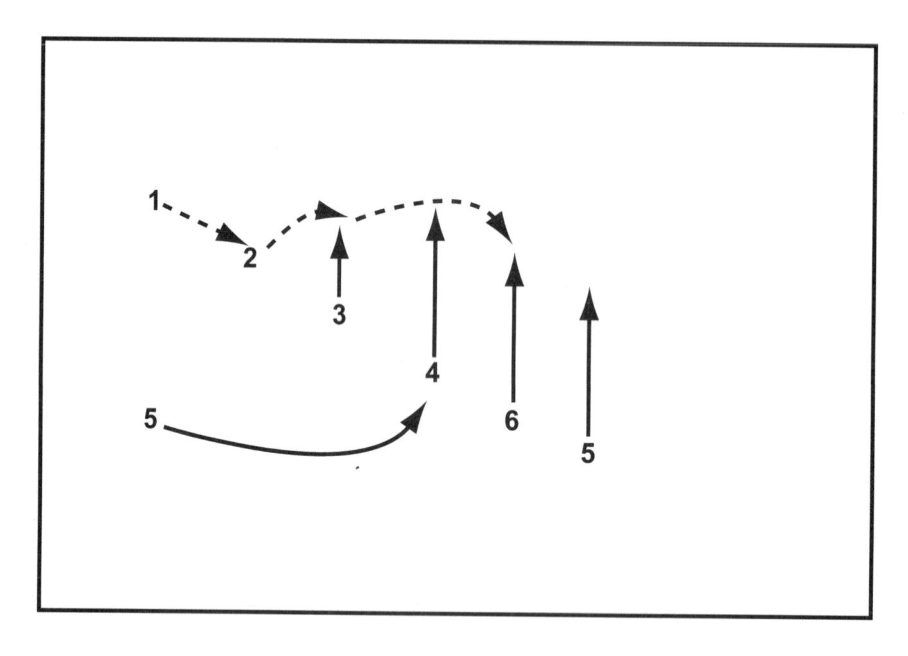

INSTRUCTIONS:

- The scrum half passes the ball to the fly half.
- The fly half passes to the inside center.
- The inside center misses the outside center and hits the fullback coming into the line.
- The blind-side winger covers for the fullback.

COACHING POINTS:

- Emphasize running from depth.
- After the outside center has been missed, that player should loop to support the play.

70 2-3 SWITCH

OBJECTIVE: Back play
NUMBER OF PLAYERS: 7
AREA/FIELD: Half field (up to full field)
TIME: 7–8 minutes
EQUIPMENT: 1 ball

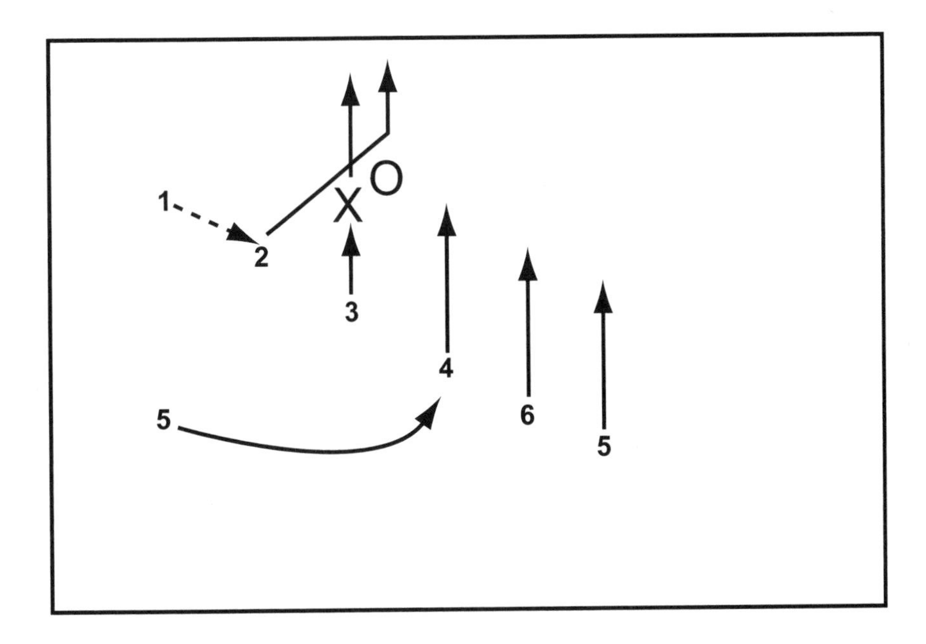

INSTRUCTIONS:

- The scrum half passes the ball to the fly half.
- The fly half runs across the path of the inside center, turns clockwise, and gives the ball to the inside center, bursting on the inside.

COACHING POINTS:

- Emphasize the need for backs to run straight (often there's a tendency to drift wide).

71 2-4 DRIFT

OBJECTIVE: Back play
NUMBER OF PLAYERS: 7
AREA/FIELD: Half field (up to full field)
TIME: 7–8 minutes
EQUIPMENT: 1 ball

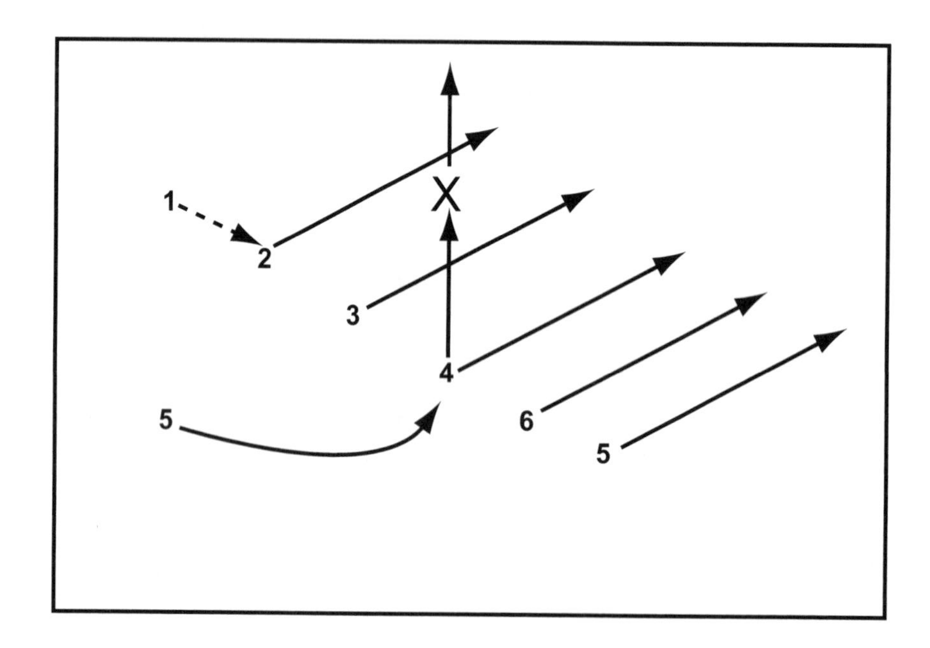

INSTRUCTIONS:

- The scrum half passes the ball to the fly half.
- The fly half and scrum half drift across the field and maintain spacing.
- The outside center takes the ball at pace from the fly half (switch inside).
- The outside center crashes or links outside.

COACHING POINTS:

- Emphasize the effectiveness of this play for times when the opposition overplays the angle of attack.

72 5 IN

OBJECTIVE: Back play

NUMBER OF PLAYERS: 7

AREA/FIELD: Half field (up to full field)

TIME: 7–8 minutes

EQUIPMENT: 1 ball

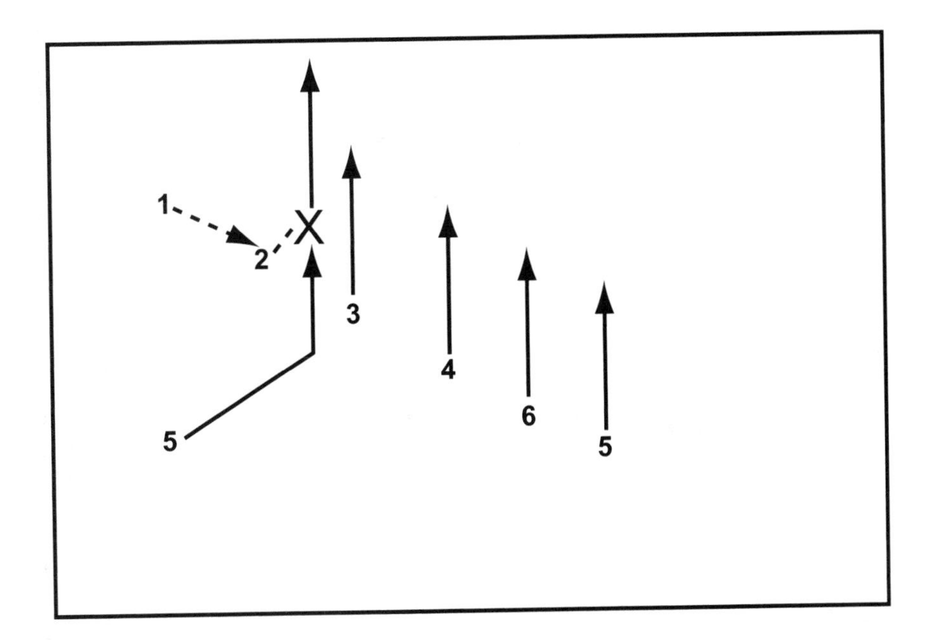

INSTRUCTIONS:

- The scrum half passes the ball to the fly half.
- The fly half pops the pass to the blind-side winger on the burst.
- The blind-side winger hits the gap, then looks for outside support.
- The fly half loops outside to create overlap.

COACHING POINTS:

- This play should be run from a scrum.

73 WING IN THE CENTERS

OBJECTIVE: Back play
NUMBER OF PLAYERS: 7
AREA/FIELD: Half field (up to full field)
TIME: 7–8 minutes
EQUIPMENT: 1 ball

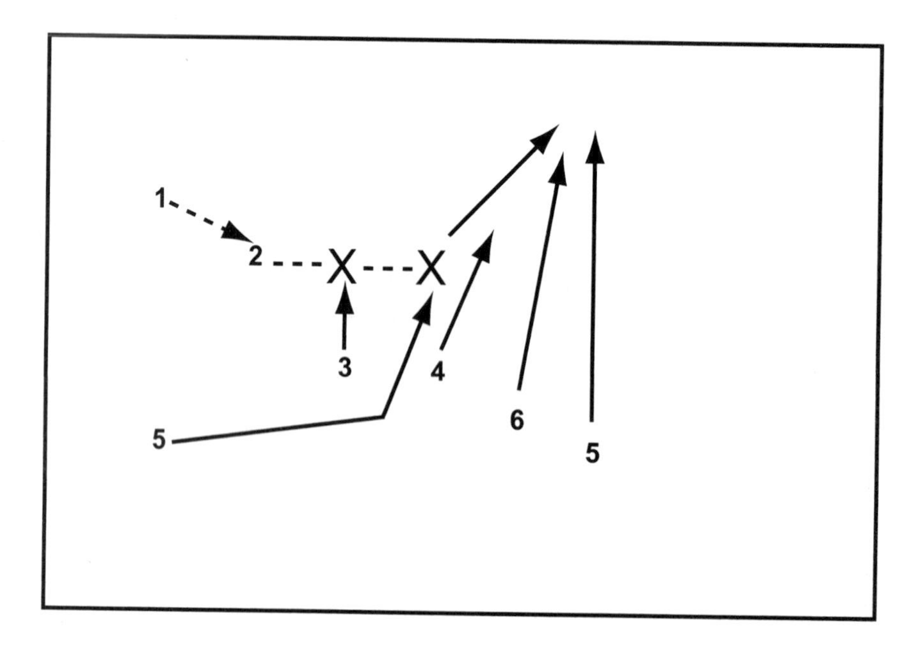

INSTRUCTIONS:

- The scrum half passes the ball to the fly half.
- The fly half moves the ball to the inside center with a quick pass.
- The inside center pops the ball to the blind-side winger on the burst.
- The winger shoots the gap between the opposing centers or crashes on the opposing outside center and looks to pop the ball to the supporting players.

74 3-5 D

OBJECTIVE: Back play

NUMBER OF PLAYERS: 7

AREA/FIELD: Half field (up to full field)

TIME: 7–8 minutes

EQUIPMENT: 1 ball

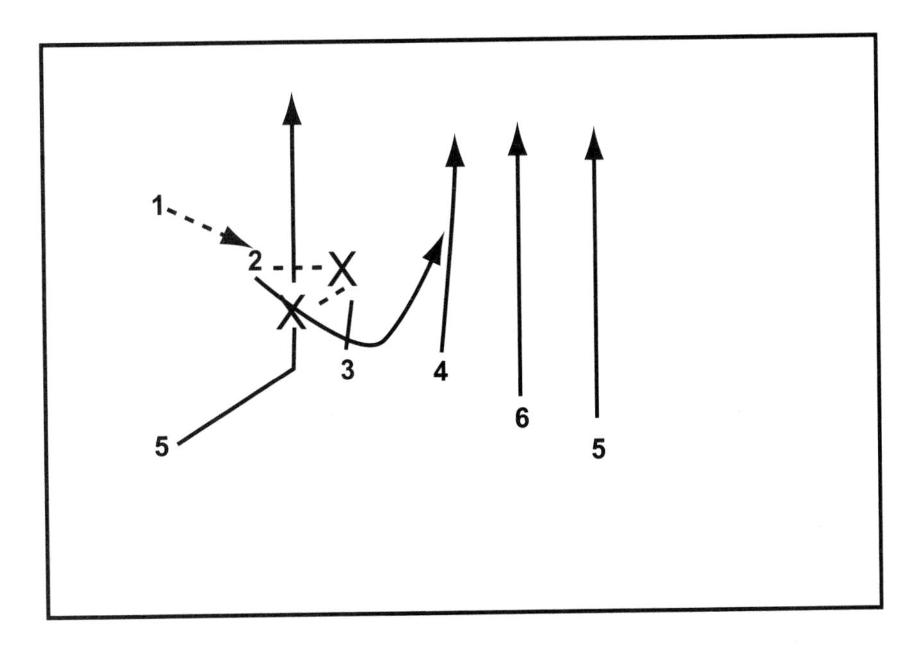

INSTRUCTIONS:

- The scrum half passes the ball to the fly half.
- The fly half pops the pass to the inside center, then loops.
- The inside center fakes the pass to the fly half, then turns clockwise and hits the blind-side winger on the inside.
- The winger looks to link outside.

COACHING POINTS:

- This play focuses on timing and works well against a poor tackling fly half.

75 SUNBURST

OBJECTIVE: Back play

NUMBER OF PLAYERS: 7

AREA/FIELD: Half field (up to full field)

TIME: 7–8 minutes

EQUIPMENT: 1 ball

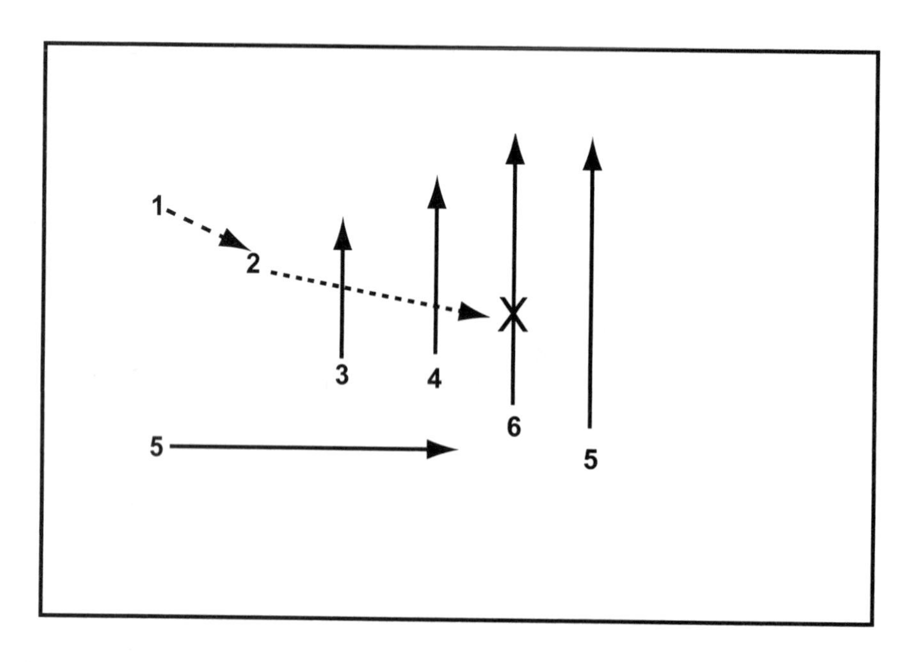

INSTRUCTIONS:

- The scrum half passes the ball to the fly half.
- The fly half hits the fullback, missing the inside and outside centers.
- The inside center, outside center, and blind-side winger support the play.
- The blind-side winger covers for the fullback.

76

PIVOT 4-5

OBJECTIVE: Back play
NUMBER OF PLAYERS: 7
AREA/FIELD: Half field (up to full field)
TIME: 7–8 minutes
EQUIPMENT: 1 ball

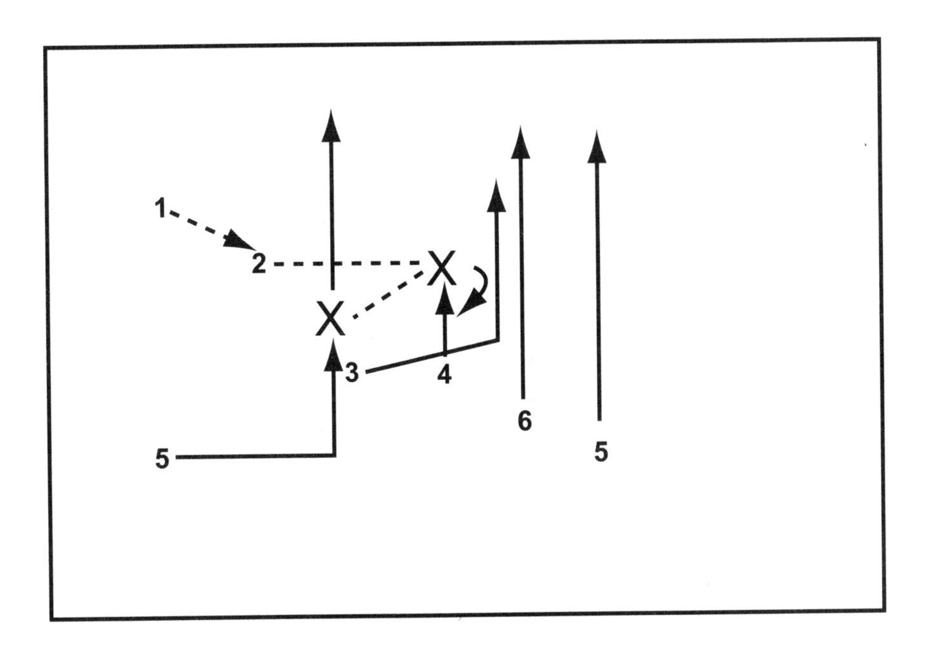

INSTRUCTIONS:

- The scrum half passes the ball to the fly half.
- The fly half misses the inside center and hits the outside center.
- The inside center leaves as the fly half gets the ball from the scrum half.
- The inside center loops the outside center, a couple of meters off hip.
- The outside center fakes the pass to the inside center, turns in a clockwise direction, fakes the pass to the fly half, and then hits the winger on the inside.
- The winger shoots the gap, then looks to link with the fly half.

77 PIVOT 4-2

OBJECTIVE: Back play
NUMBER OF PLAYERS: 7
AREA/FIELD: Half field (up to full field)
TIME: 7–8 minutes
EQUIPMENT: 1 ball

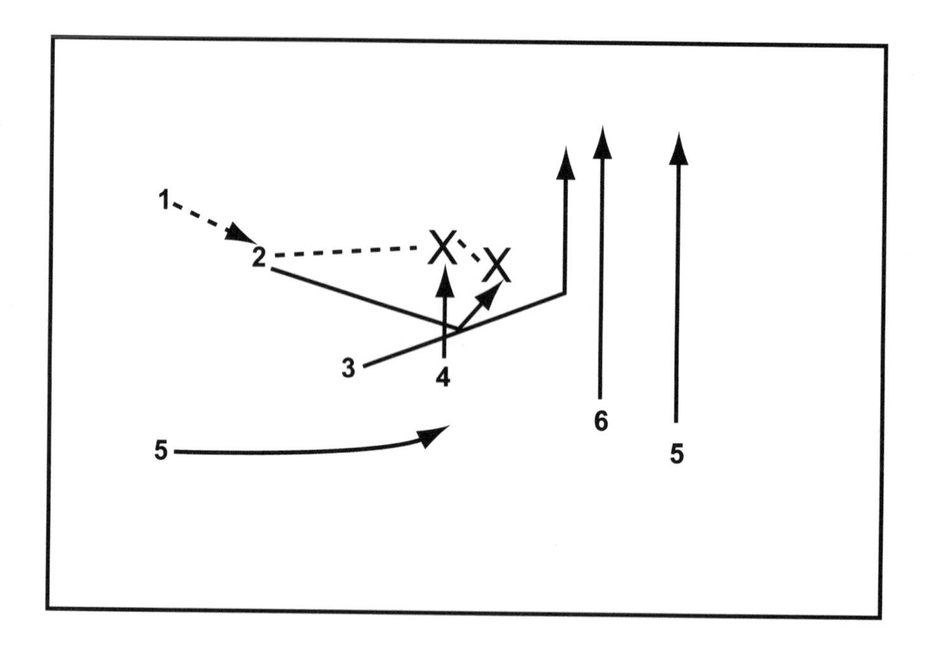

INSTRUCTIONS:

- The scrum half passes the ball to the fly half.
- The fly half misses the inside center and hits the outside center.
- The inside center leaves as the fly half gets the ball from the scrum half.
- The fly half loops the outside center, a couple of meters off hip.
- The outside center fakes the pass to the inside center, then hits the fly half off hip.
- The fly half straightens, then looks for support to the outside.
- The fullback and the winger give support.
- The blind-side winger covers for the fullback.

78 WING FLARE (FULLBACK FLARE)

OBJECTIVE: Back play
NUMBER OF PLAYERS: 7
AREA/FIELD: Half field (up to full field)
TIME: 7–8 minutes
EQUIPMENT: 1 ball

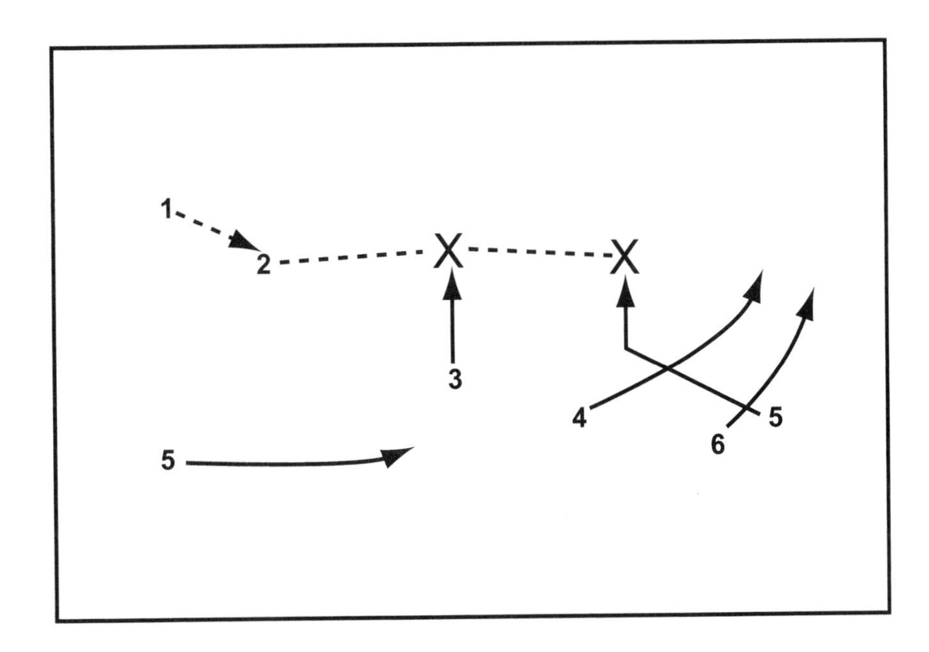

INSTRUCTIONS:

- The scrum half passes the ball to the fly half.
- The fly half passes to the inside center.
- The outside center drifts across the winger's path.
- The winger cuts back, receives the pass from the inside center, then shoots the gap created by the flare.
- The fullback and outside center provide support to the outside.
- The blind-side winger covers for the fullback.

COACHING POINTS:

- Running with the fullback instead of the winger is an option.

79 SCISSORS

OBJECTIVE: Back play
NUMBER OF PLAYERS: 7
AREA/FIELD: Half field (up to full field)
TIME: 7–8 minutes
EQUIPMENT: 1 ball

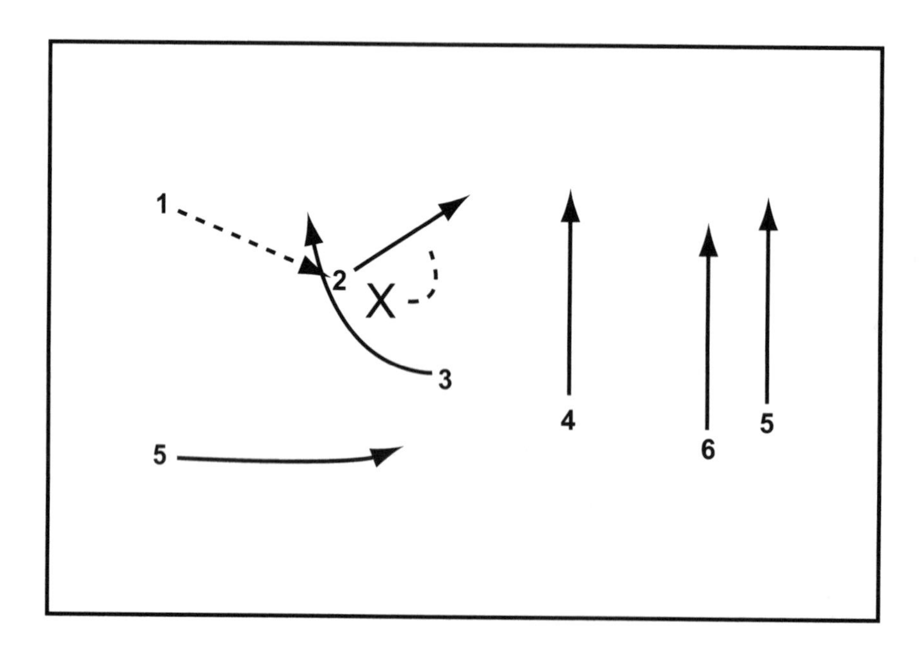

INSTRUCTIONS:

- The scrum half passes the ball to the fly half.
- The fly half runs diagonally across the field.
- The inside center runs diagonally also, but at the last moment cuts behind the fly half.
- The ball should be handed off.
- The players form an X pattern.

COACHING POINTS:

- This maneuver can be run using any combination of backs.

80 DUMMY SCISSORS (3 GIVE TO 4)

OBJECTIVE: Back play
NUMBER OF PLAYERS: 7
AREA/FIELD: Half field (up to full field)
TIME: 7–8 minutes
EQUIPMENT: 1 ball

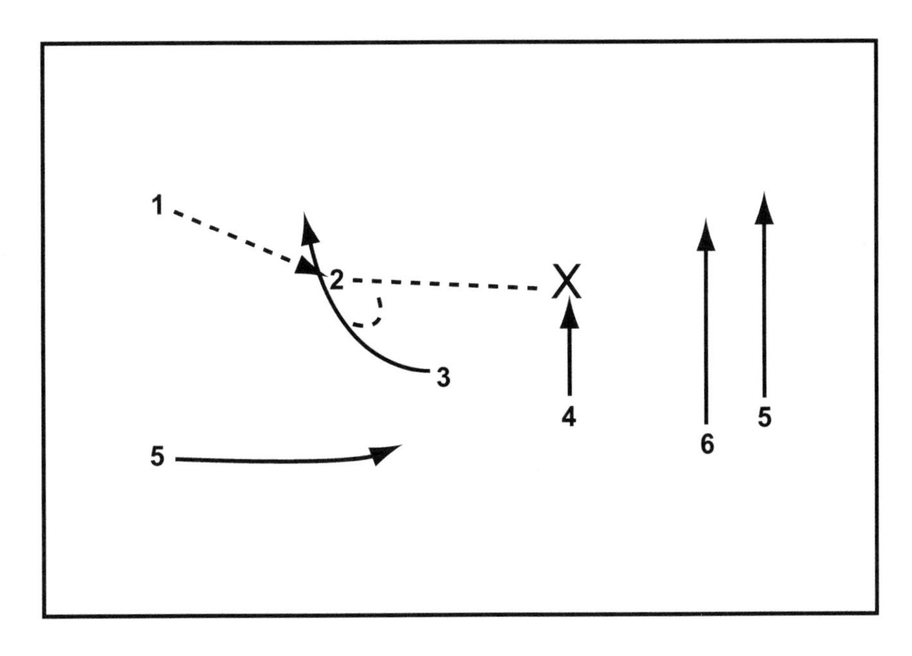

INSTRUCTIONS:

- The scrum half passes the ball to the fly half.
- The fly half runs diagonally across the field, then fakes the scissor move (shown in Drill 13) with the inside center.
- The inside center should bend at the waist and call for the ball to carry out the fake.
- The fly half continues and completes a scissor move with the next back (the outside center).

81 6-5 SWITCH

OBJECTIVE: Back play
NUMBER OF PLAYERS: 7
AREA/FIELD: Half field (up to full field)
TIME: 7–8 minutes
EQUIPMENT: 1 ball

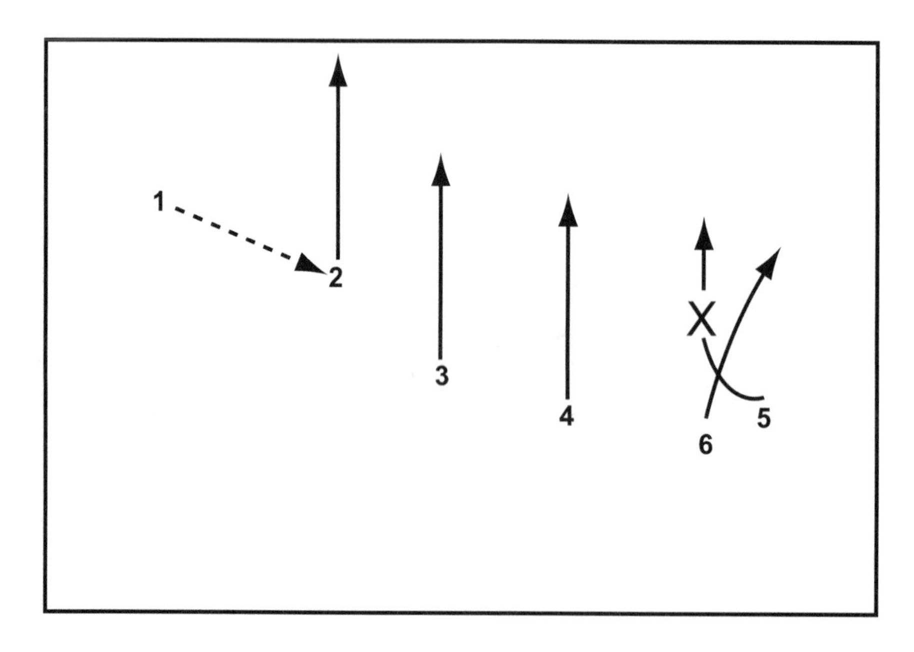

INSTRUCTIONS:
- When the ball moves through the hands of the backs, the fullback runs diagonally toward the sidelines.
- Before running into touch, the player switch-passes with 5.
- The fullback first looks outside, then turns his whole body to look inside and simply passes to the winger who is cutting back into the field.

COACHING POINTS:
- This maneuver is effective at keeping the ball in play.

82 CHIP KICK

OBJECTIVE: Back play

NUMBER OF PLAYERS: 7

AREA/FIELD: Half field (up to full field)

TIME: 7–8 minutes

EQUIPMENT: 1 ball

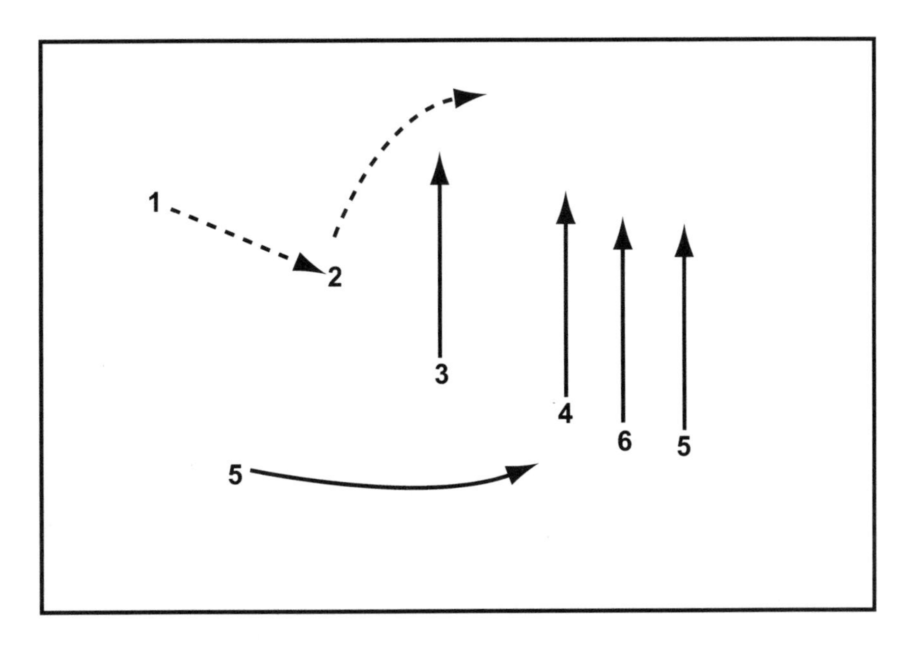

INSTRUCTIONS:

- The attacking player delivers a short chip kick over the head of the opposition; the player runs hard in an attempt to regain possession of the ball.

COACHING POINTS:

- This kick is especially effective if the opposition closes in quickly.

83 GRUB KICK

OBJECTIVE: Back play
NUMBER OF PLAYERS: 7
AREA/FIELD: Half field (up to full field)
TIME: 7–8 minutes
EQUIPMENT: 1 ball

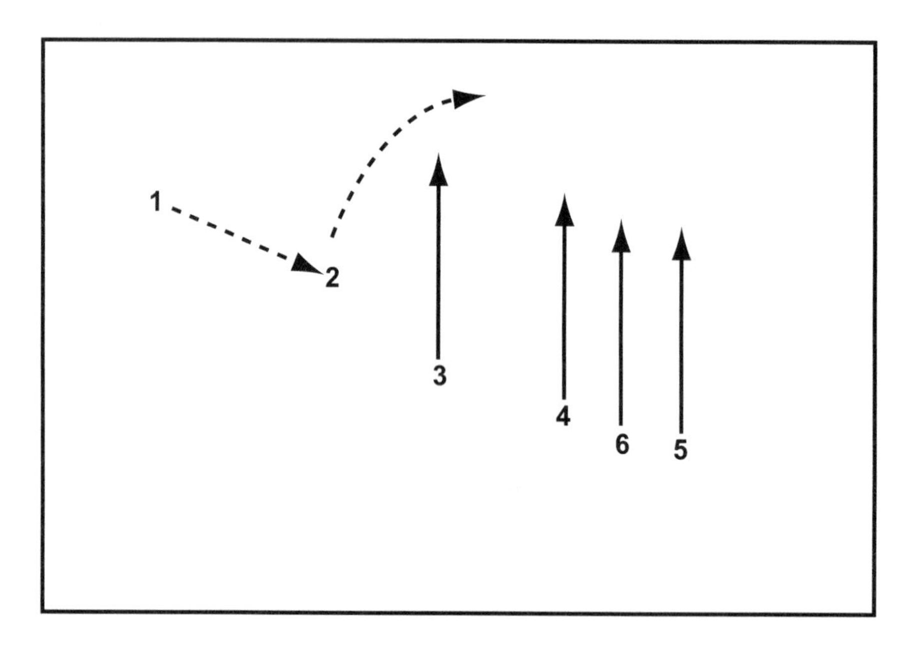

INSTRUCTIONS:

- The attacking player delivers a low kick that rolls along the ground and should travel approximately 10–15 meters.
- The player tries to angle the kick through the gap between opposing players.

COACHING POINTS:

- The player next to the kicker will often recover the ball.
- If the ball is kicked properly, it will bounce a few times, making it possible to catch the ball on a hop.

84 UP AND UNDER

OBJECTIVE: Back play
NUMBER OF PLAYERS: 7
AREA/FIELD: Half field (up to full field)
TIME: 7–8 minutes
EQUIPMENT: 1 ball

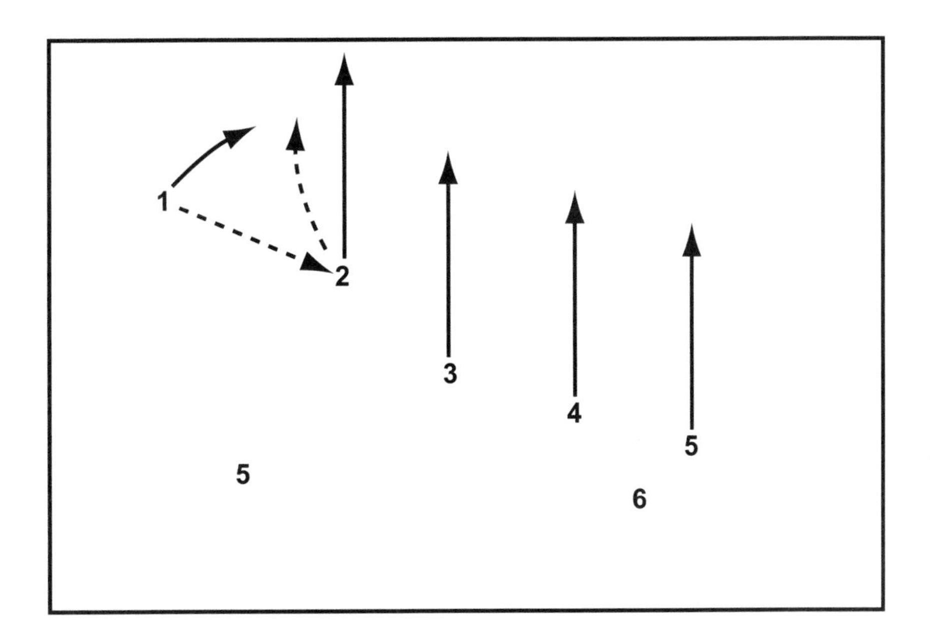

INSTRUCTIONS:

- The attacking player delivers a high kick (up and under kick) that should travel at least 20 meters.
- The kick is designed to pressure the opponent.
- The backs wait for the kick (the line is often flat rather than steep).
- Defensive backs, including the kicker, run down and try to tackle the catcher in an attempt to regain possession of the ball.

COACHING POINTS:

- The fly half generally does most of the kicking for the backs.
- The fly half may elect to use a "call" to let his backs and forwards know what is happening; a commonly used system involves dividing the field into three areas (i.e., RFC/R — a kick to the far left side, /F — a kick to the center, and /C — a kick to the far right side).

FORWARD PLAY

Many drills found in Chapter 3 (Contact Drills) will prove useful for forward training.

POINTS TO CONSIDER

This chapter covers the basics of forward play. Forwards can win possession of the ball through lineouts and scrumming (rucking and mauling). Therefore, some of the most common and useful drills for practicing forward play are live lineouts and scrums.

A lineout takes place when the ball goes out-of-bounds. In this situation, forwards attempt to win possession of the ball when it is thrown in from the sidelines.The scrum is made up of eight players who attempt to push the opposition back in hopes of winning the ball.

Keep in mind that even when drilling these set configurations it is important to involve some degree of running. Such movement could be accomplished by having players chase a loose ball on the field or simply having players run back and forth across the field to add an extra element of aerobic conditioning. The point cannot be stressed enough: fitness must be worked on throughout each practice session.

A quality fitness standard is a must for the forward position.The main responsibility of this player is to follow the ball for the full extent of the game and win or maintain possession. In order to accomplish this, it becomes important for these players to work as a unit and give support to the ball. The team that has the greater number of forwards arriving at the breakdown (contact point) will most likely be the team to come away with the ball. Also, when backs get caught up in the breakdown (ruck or maul), the forwards must be able to give support and fill in.

A coach can choose to practice set pieces against a token defense, against a scrum machine, or against full opposition. Running planned scenarios from set pieces can prove to be a very effective drill strategy. For example, a coach may wish to place opponents in various locations in order to predetermine what resulting action will take place.

Again, it is recommended that a coach build in other drills to complement practice sessions involving set pieces. After all, forwards must have the endurance to arrive at the scrum or lineout and still add to the play. Forwards must attempt to win and secure their own possession while at the same time attempting to steal and spoil the opponents' possession.

POSITIONAL REQUIREMENTS

Each forward position has its own unique characteristics. With experience, a player better understands how to develop those characteristics.

PROP

The following are the positional requirements of the prop:

- strong upper-body strength (usually this player will be a shorter/stockier athlete)
- effective participation in set pieces (scrummages and lineouts)
- ability to add to the play in the rucks and mauls
- loose head responsible for supporting the hooker and assisting in gaining the put-in
- tight head responsible for disrupting the opposition loose head and hooker

HOOKER

The following are the positional requirements of the hooker:

- possesses attributes/skills similar to those of the prop
- flexibility to allow for greater range of motion
- ability to effectively and accurately throw the ball into the lineout
- ability to deliver a quick strike to win possession of the ball

LOCK

The following are the positional requirements of the lock:

- size/strength/height (the lock is often the largest player on the field)
- ability to provide the lineout with height and the scrum with push
- ability to add to the play in set pieces

BACK ROW

The following are the positional requirements of the back row:

- possesses all-around rugby skills
- demonstrated speed
- excellent tackling skills
- proven ball-winning and retention skills
- advanced tactical decision-making skills (back-row players will have their hands on the ball often)

LINEOUT PLAYS

A lineout is the means of restarting play when the ball has gone into touch. The basic skills that are utilized include throwing, catching, jumping, lifting, and supporting. Essentially, nine players work together to gain possession of the ball. A lineout must have at least two players in the line but may not contain more than seven. The scrum half position coordinates the link with the backs. One thing to keep in mind—it is essential that the player throwing the ball in from the sidelines be capable of throwing the ball on target.

I will briefly describe three common systems used to let your team know where the ball is going. Keep in mind that these are basic plays and should be practiced often. A team wants to have the ability to move the ball without the opposition predicting the strategy of the approach. It should be the team goal to win all its possessions and steal the opponents' ball as often as possible.

LIVE NUMBER

Using a "live number" means that a predetermined number is initially set among team members before the game. Then, when a player calls out a group of numbers, the number that directly follows the live number is the play or the designated jumper that the throw is going to. For example, if the live number is "7" and the player calls out "45 72 35," then the play is going to be represented by the number 2.

LETTER SYSTEM

Using a letter system follows a logic similar to that found with the live number system. Words rather than numbers are used as decoys in this case, however. Assume that a team uses the letter system "TIN CAN." In this case, any word that begins with a "T" goes to the first jumper, any word that begins with an "I" goes to the second jumper, and so on.

HAND/BODY POSITION SIGNALS

Using hand and body position signaling requires that the team devise a series of positions or movements. These signals represent instructions for the team to carry out. For example, the hands held together may indicate that the throw is going to go to the first jumper, or a balled fist may signal that the second jumper will receive the throw. The scrum half would be the player who gives the signals and therefore relays the play at hand to the rest of the team.

BASIC LINEOUT THROWS

Now let's discuss basic types of lineout throws. These should provide a coach with a fair overview of the common plays used at a lineout. With a solid foundation of basic plays a coach can take this information and create other plays. My endorsement is this: *Keep it Simple Silly*. Remember that it is always better to run a few plays well than it is to run several plays poorly. Here are a few general points to consider:

- teams commonly throw to the number 2, 4, or 6 player in the lineout (lineout rules allow players to be lifted)
- throwing to a jumper demands that another player support that catch by ripping the ball (usually 5 assists the 2nd jumper and 2 rips for the 4th jumper)
- teams should work on catching or tapping the ball
- solid binding between players in the lineout is critical
- practice makes perfect

OVER THE TOP

This is a play where the ball is simply thrown over the entire lineout and the player at the end attempts to run and catch it.

BACK PEEL

In this play the ball is thrown to the back jumper (usually position 6). A player from the front of the line leaves as the ball is thrown and runs along the line. This player tries to catch the tapped ball, then turns and runs at the fly half. The trailing players support the play. It is important to make sure that the backs are aware when this play has been called so that they are able to support the run.

FRONT PEEL

This play is similar to the back peel except that the players run up along the sideline. The number 2 jumper taps the ball down to a player running from the back of the lineout, and this player immediately turns upfield and runs up the sideline with supporters in tow.

THE SHORT QUICK ONE

In this play the player throwing the ball in places the ball on the ground and then quickly flips it to the first person in the lineout (remember, the ball must be passed infield 5 meters). A team will often use this play to catch the opponent napping. It is also commonly used in lineouts that are close to the goal line and to attack the blind side (short side) of the field.

SHORT LINEOUTS

Short lineouts are often useful to keep the opponent on its toes. Sometimes they are used if your team is not strong in full lineouts. The initial setup of the players is to have the first jumper line up 6 meters from the sideline. The second jumper should be 7 or 8 meters directly behind. This is the basic setup from which all plays are run. Remember, basic throws to the first or second jumper are standard plays. On the following pages I will describe four additional plays and include diagrams.

85 OVER THE TOP

OBJECTIVE: To win possession of the ball
NUMBER OF PLAYERS: 4
AREA/FIELD: 20 yards × 20 yards
TIME: 5 minutes
EQUIPMENT: 1 ball

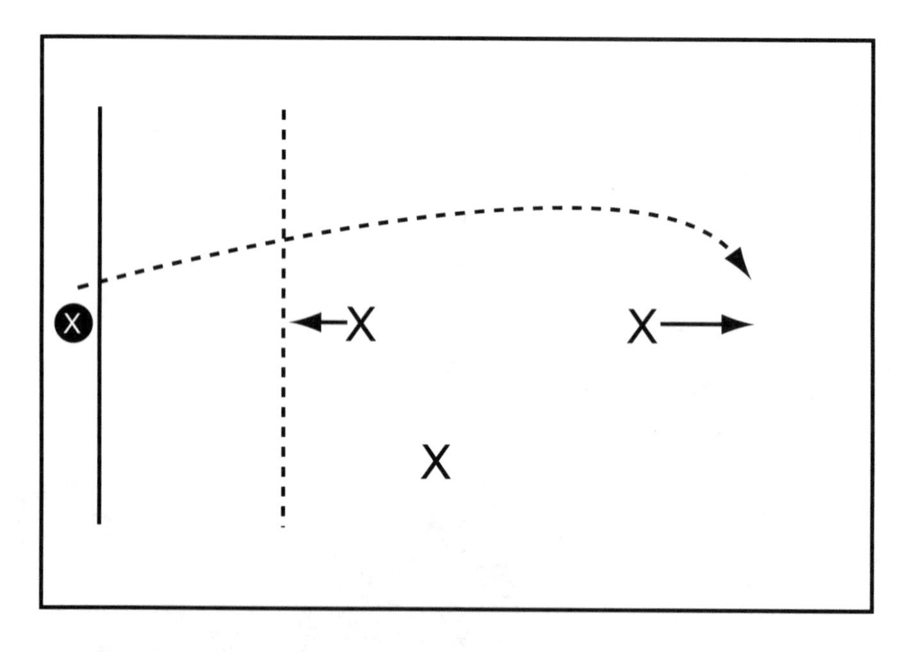

INSTRUCTIONS:
- The first jumper runs forward as the ball is thrown into the field of play.
- The second jumper moves back and receives the long throw over the top.

COACHING POINTS:
- Play is less effective in windy playing conditions.

86 TO THE FRONT

OBJECTIVE: To win possession of the ball

NUMBER OF PLAYERS: 4

AREA/FIELD: 20 yards × 20 yards

TIME: 5 minutes

EQUIPMENT: 1 ball

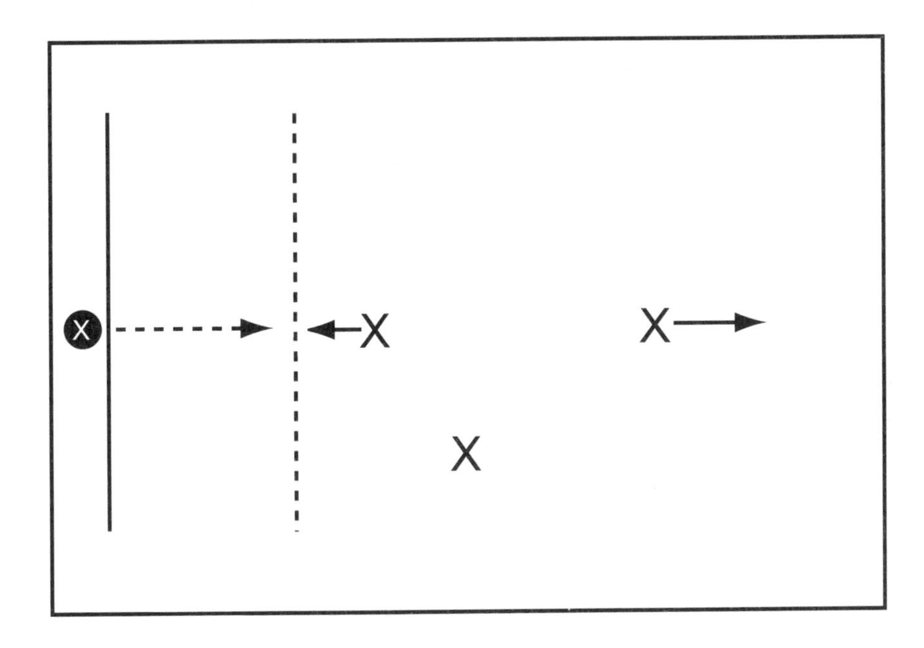

INSTRUCTIONS:

- The second jumper moves back as the ball is thrown into the field of play.
- The first jumper runs forward to catch the quick pass thrown in.

COACHING POINTS:

- The ball is often given right back to the player who threw the ball in.

87 IN THE MIDDLE

OBJECTIVE: To win possession of the ball
NUMBER OF PLAYERS: 4
AREA/FIELD: 20 yards × 20 yards
TIME: 5 minutes
EQUIPMENT: 1 ball

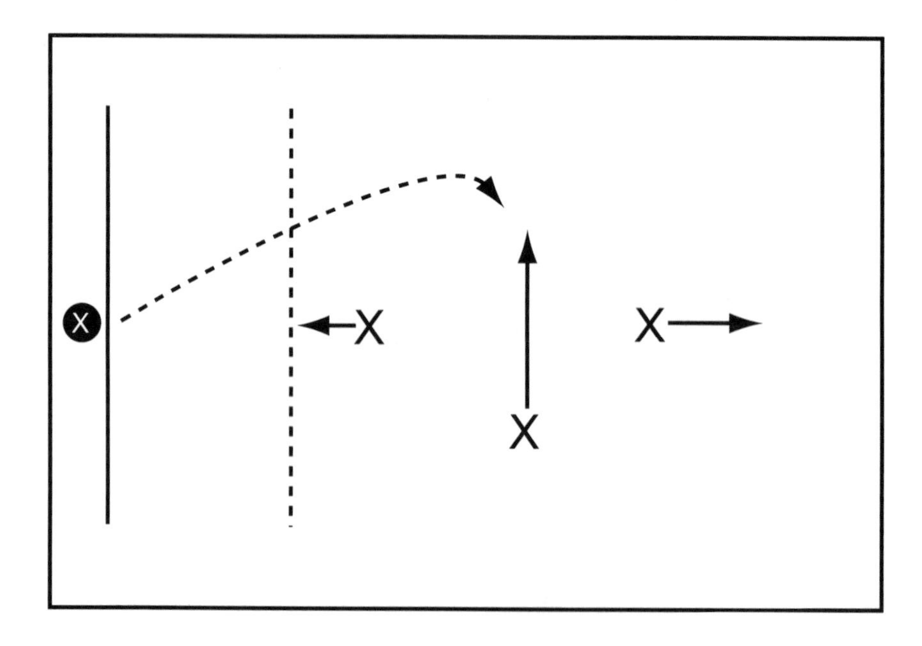

INSTRUCTIONS:

- The first jumper runs forward.
- The back jumper moves backward as the ball is thrown.
- The toss is directed to the gap in between the two players.
- The scrum half catches the ball and drives into the opponents.
- Supporting forwards run up to secure possession.

88 THE SWITCH

OBJECTIVE: To win possession of the ball
NUMBER OF PLAYERS: 4
AREA/FIELD: 20 yards × 20 yards
TIME: 5 minutes
EQUIPMENT: 1 ball

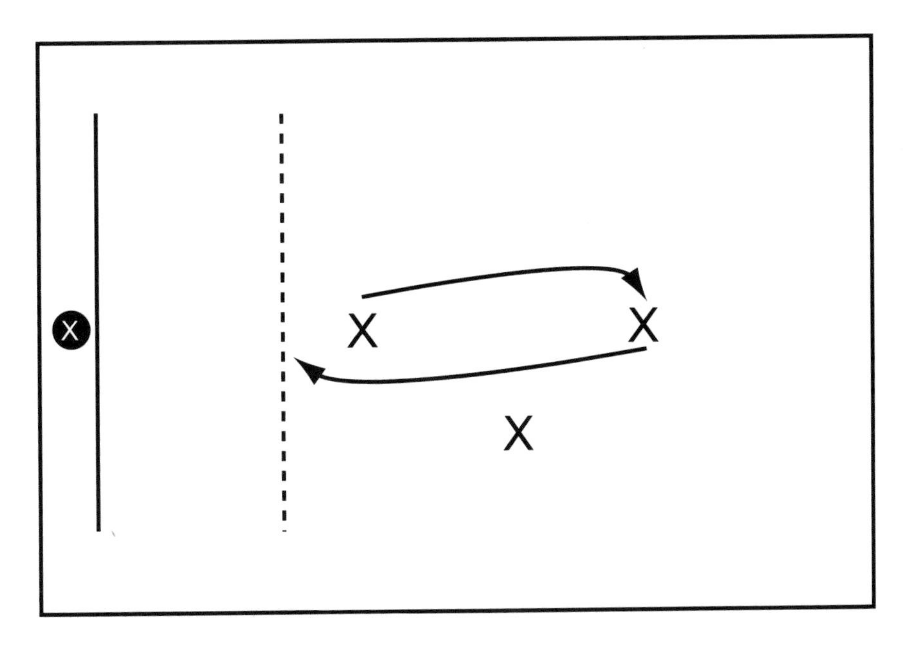

INSTRUCTIONS:

- The front and back jumpers switch positions as the ball is being thrown into the field of play.
- The players brush shoulders as they go by each other.
- The ball is thrown to either player.

COACHING POINTS:

- Generally, the player moving forward has more success in receiving the pass.

BACK-ROW PLAYS

Back-row plays from a scrummage are carried out by the two flankers, the number 8 player, and the scrum half. On the following pages I will describe three plays and include diagrams. These plays can be worked on against an opposing scrum, against a scrum machine, or unopposed.

89 SAMPLE PLAY 1

OBJECTIVE: Improving back-row attack

NUMBER OF PLAYERS: 9

AREA/FIELD: 25 yards × 25 yards

TIME: 5–10 minutes

EQUIPMENT: 1 ball

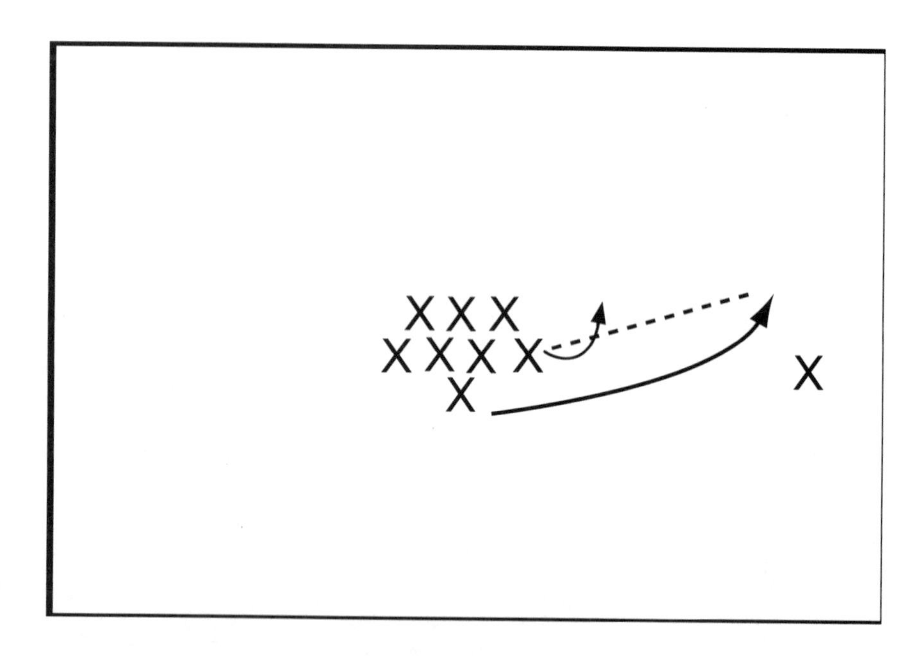

INSTRUCTIONS:

- The number 8 player picks the ball up and runs wide.
- The flanker to that side hangs back and receives an inside pass from the number 8 player.
- The scrum half stays out wide with the number 8 player.

COACHING POINTS:

- The number 8 player and scrum half attempt to draw the defenders into overcommitting.
- This play is effective inside the opponent's 10-meter line.

90 SAMPLE PLAY 2

OBJECTIVE: Improving back-row attack

NUMBER OF PLAYERS: 9

AREA/FIELD: 25 yards × 25 yards

TIME: 5–10 minutes

EQUIPMENT: 1 ball

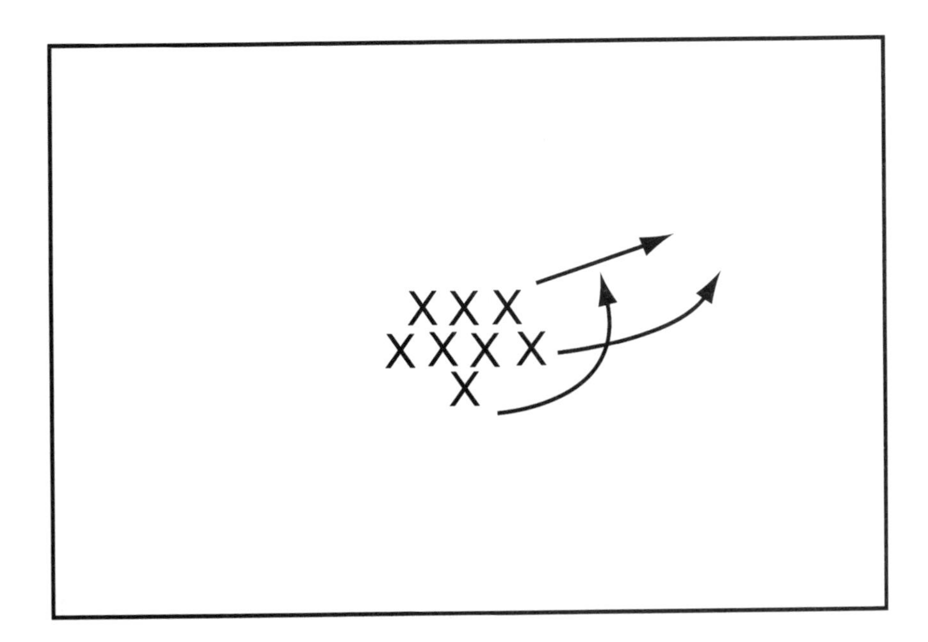

INSTRUCTIONS:

- The number 8 player picks the ball up and runs upfield (tight to the scrum).
- At first contact the number 8 player hands the ball off to the flanker on the scrum side.
- The scrum half gives support out wide to the flanker.

COACHING POINTS:

- This play is designed to create an overlap by drawing opposing backs into a tackle situation.

91 SAMPLE PLAY 3

OBJECTIVE: Improving back-row attack

NUMBER OF PLAYERS: 9

AREA/FIELD: 25 yards × 25 yards

TIME: 5–10 minutes

EQUIPMENT: 1 ball

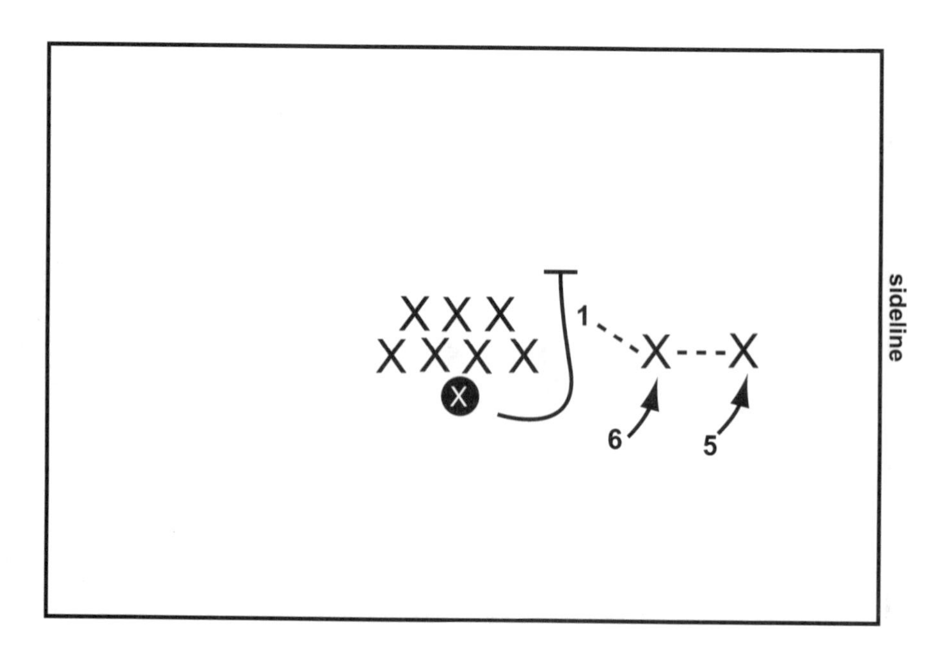

INSTRUCTIONS:

- The number 8 player picks the ball up and runs into contact.
- The closest flanker sets the maul and rips the ball.
- The scrum half calls for the quick ball and carries on with the fullback and winger.

COACHING POINTS:

- This play is often used to attack the blind side (short side) of the field.

FITNESS

Fitness enhancement should be a major focus of drill work throughout practice sessions.

92 PAIR SPRINT

OBJECTIVE: Improving fitness

NUMBER OF PLAYERS: 10 (to unlimited)

AREA/FIELD: Full field

TIME: 8–15 minutes

EQUIPMENT: 4 pylons

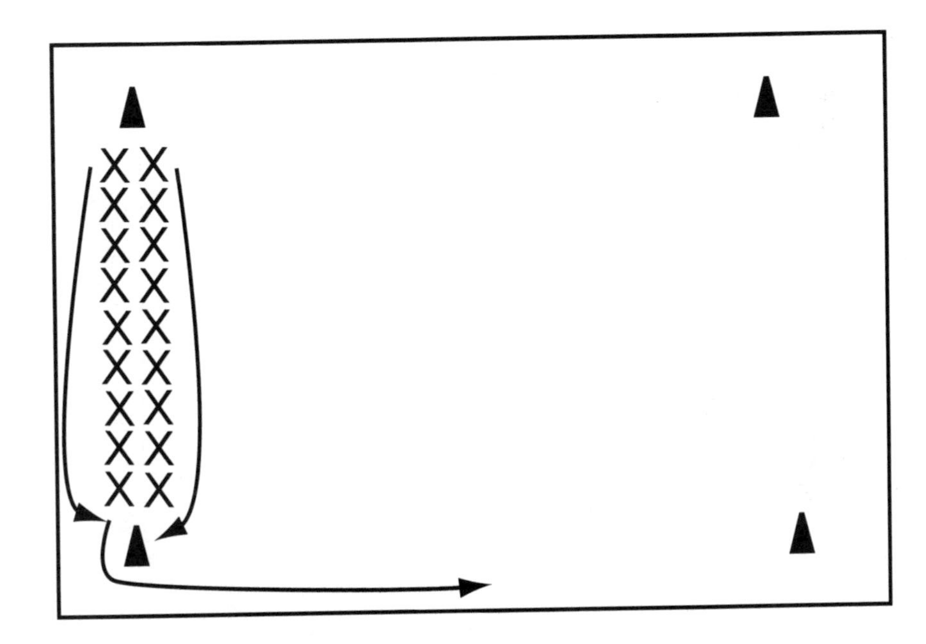

INSTRUCTIONS:

- Players circle the outside of the field in two single-file lines.
- Each player pairs up with the adjacent runner from the other line.
- When a whistle sounds, the rearmost pair split to each side and sprint to the front of each respective line.

COACHING POINTS:

- The coach may choose to reduce the size of the running area.

93 6-MINUTE DRILL

OBJECTIVE: Improving fitness

NUMBER OF PLAYERS: 1 (to unlimited)

AREA/FIELD: Full field

TIME: 6–15 minutes

EQUIPMENT: None

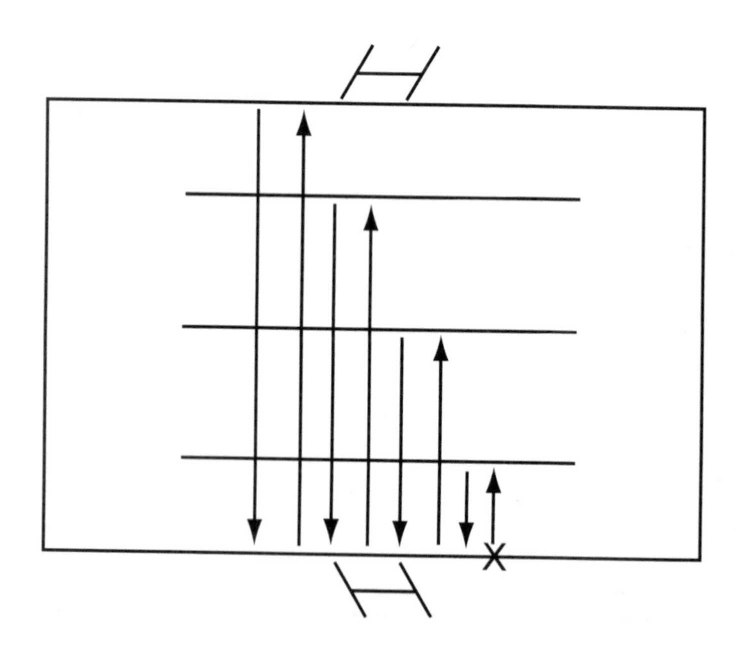

INSTRUCTIONS:

- Each player runs from the goal line to the near 22-meter line and back; then to the center line and back; then to the far 22-meter line and back; then to the the far goal line and back.
- Players attempt to complete this routine three times in a 6-minute time period.

COACHING POINTS:

- Make sure that players warm-up properly before this activity and stretch after completion.
- If a large number of players are finishing at or near the 6-minute mark, team fitness level is high.
- Compare the team fitness level at preseason, mid-season, and at season's end—there should clearly be improvement.

94 PYRAMID SHUTTLE

OBJECTIVE: Improving fitness
NUMBER OF PLAYERS: Groups of 3 (to unlimited)
AREA/FIELD: Full field
TIME: 8–20 minutes
EQUIPMENT: 1 ball (per group)

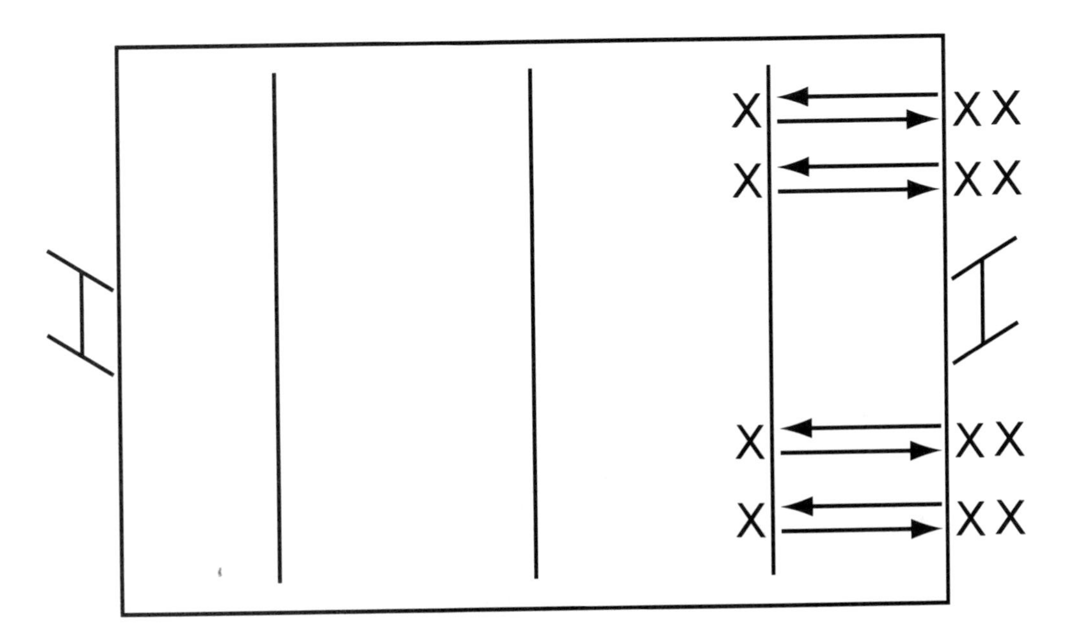

INSTRUCTIONS:

- Players spread out along the goal line in groups.
- A player from each group walks out to the 22-meter line; a player on the goal line runs out to this player.
- The groups shuttle the designated length.
- Players complete a number of runs for each length.
- The single player moves back to the center line and the shuttle continues (the far 22-meter line and the goal line may also be used).

COACHING POINTS:

- A common number of runs set in this drill are: 10-8-4-2 (per player).
- This drill imitates the stop-and-go aspect of the game.
- Players may use a ball to hand off between group members at each shuttle length.

95 SQUARE DRILL

OBJECTIVE: Improving fitness
NUMBER OF PLAYERS: 1 (to unlimited)
AREA/FIELD: Half field (up to full field)
TIME: Variable
EQUIPMENT: 4 pylons

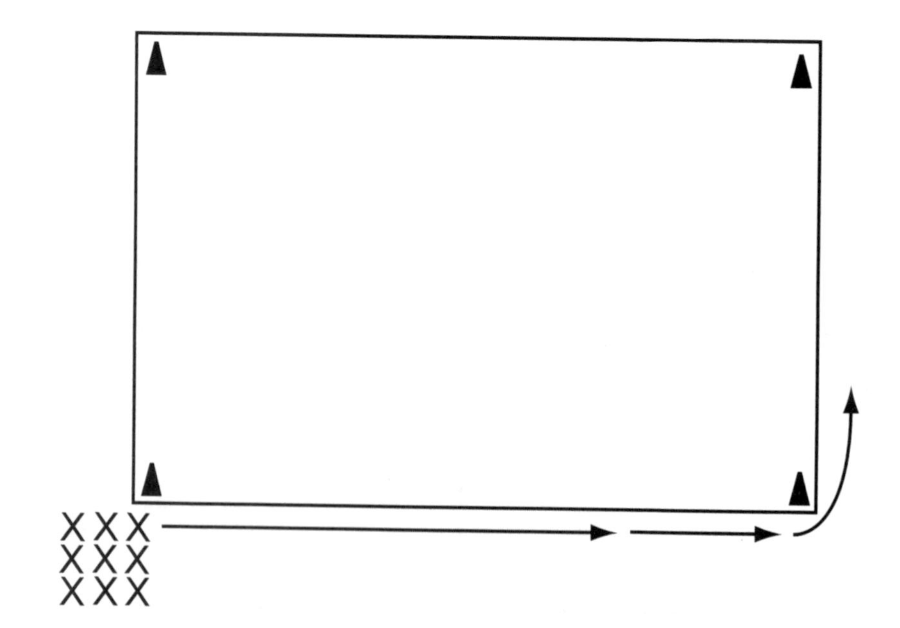

INSTRUCTIONS:

- Players run around a square area.
- Players start at one corner of the square and sprint one side, then jog three.
- Players then sprint two sides and jog two sides.
- Players then sprint three sides and jog one side.
- Players then sprint around all four sides of the square.

COACHING POINTS:

- Coach may time player results and set team and individual goals based on performance.

96 WIND SPRINTS

OBJECTIVE: Improving fitness
NUMBER OF PLAYERS: 1 (to unlimited)
AREA/FIELD: 30 yards × 30 yards
TIME: 5–15 minutes
EQUIPMENT: 6 pylons

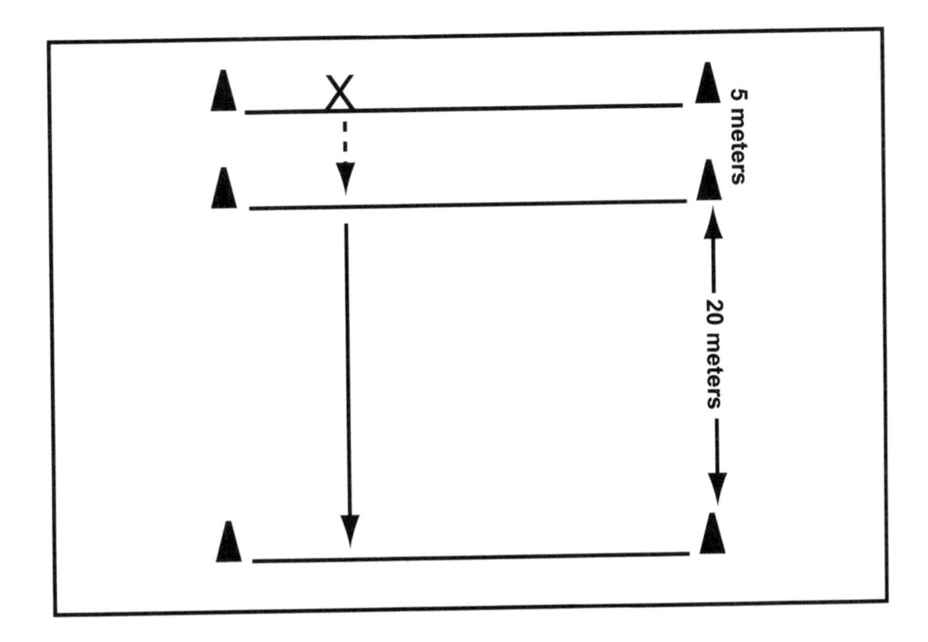

INSTRUCTIONS:
- Players jog 5 meters, then sprint hard for 20 meters.
- Players rest for 5 seconds and then repeat.

COACHING POINTS:
- Players may carry a ball or pass a ball between other runners during this drill.

97 HILL WORK

OBJECTIVE: Improving fitness
NUMBER OF PLAYERS: 1 (to unlimited)
AREA/FIELD: Area with an incline
TIME: 5–15 minutes
EQUIPMENT: 2 pylons

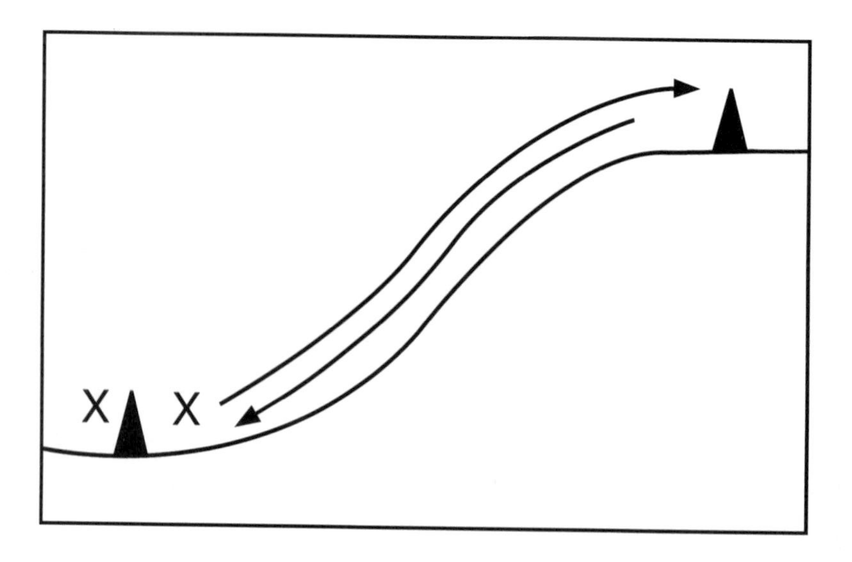

INSTRUCTIONS:
- Players run a given distance up and down an incline.

COACHING POINTS:
- Groups of three allow for appropriate recovery time between runs.
- Coaches may time player results or set a specific number of repetitions up and down the incline.

SAMPLE PRACTICE PLANS

OUTDOOR TRAINING

Daily practice is strongly advised. Do keep in mind, however, that the length of each practice session should not exceed 1.5 hours. The key is to use time effectively and carefully plan each practice session to achieve the results desired. Please note that an occasional day off in the course of a heavy playing schedule is advised. This is left up to the individual coach.

The following notes are vital points for a coach to consider when putting together a practice plan. Provided is an overview of a typical practice session, including examples of appropriate drills. Players may choose to arrive early or stay late in order to work on individual skills.

10–15 Minutes: Warm-Up

It is important to include an adequate warm-up session for players before any practice session begins.

- Try to motivate players to arrive early to begin to warm up and work on specific skills such as passing or kicking.
- A full-body warm-up should be carried out and involve all players.
- Sample stretching routine—run a ballhandling drill that involves light continuous running (a drill such as "Back and Forth").
- Players should just begin to break a sweat before a stretching routine begins. Appropriate stretches include: neck rotations, arm circles, trunk rotations, triceps stretches, hamstring stretches, quadriceps stretches, calf stretches, side lunges, groin stretches, and ankle rotations. This list does not represent a complete overview of the various stretches that can be used, but it does offer a basic warm-up. Make it a point to have your players hold static stretches for a 15–20-second count.

35 Minutes: Individual Skills

Set long-term and short-term goals for player improvement when practicing individual skills.

- Practice all skills for all players.
- Consider placing three forwards and three backs together when forming groups for drills.
- Vary these drills from practice to practice. Choose appropriate drills relating to noted areas of weakness that became evident in your most recent match.
- Plan practices to build toward the next match, and do not try to master the whole game in one single practice.

Individual Skills Sample Practice (drill descriptions found in early chapters):
- 8 minutes — Crisscross
- 6 minutes — 2 on 1
- 6 minutes — In Between
- 7 minutes — 4-Team Challenge
- 8 minutes — Line Ruck

20 Minutes: Split into Backs and Forwards

The team should be split up into two basic groups—forwards and backs.

Forwards should work on the following:
- fully opposed lineouts
- fully opposed scrums
- back-row plays

Backs should work on the following:
- back plays unopposed
- back plays opposed

20 Minutes: Total Game Play

If the number of players permits the opportunity to run a full contact scrimmage, then use this portion of the practice to simulate a live game situation. Use extra players to serve as the opposition and rotate players in and out.
- be creative—set up hypothetical situations for score and field position
- set up specific situations that require extra work (for example, run two or three penalty plays in a row before moving on to something else)
- encourage players to give full effort

10 Minutes: Fitness and Cooldown

As with any rigorous exercise/physical exertion, the cooldown portion of the session is important as preventative maintenance against injury. Fitness and flexibility are genuine concerns for the athlete. Make sure that all players are involved; the cooldown is every bit as necessary as the warm-up. It is a coach's responsibility to ensure that this activity is stressed. If the coach feels that a particular practice session has been especially strenuous, however, this section of practice can be replaced with less strenuous activity.

Suggestions for cooldown include:
- general fitness work (incorporate ballhandling drills whenever possible)
- pyramid shuttle (using a ball for each group)
- light running
- stretches (led by team captain/captains)

INDOOR TRAINING

Often a coach will find that the weather prevents the possibility of practicing outdoors, especially during the winter months. Many of the drills in this book can be adapted and run indoors during the off-season. Regardless, indoor practice sessions should still not exceed 1.5 hours.

The format for indoor practice is much the same as that for outdoor sessions. Of course, there are obvious adjustments that limited space and an indoor playing surface demand. But as explained at the outset of this book, all of the drills and information set forth can be adapted to meet a variety of circumstances.

Full-field activities are impossible to run; this provides an excellent opportunity to work on individual and unit skills. Full contact is not recommended; however, modified contact and form tackling using mats can be quite effective. The fact is, indoor practice allows players to focus on team communication skills and work on specific technical adjustments.

STATION WORK

This sample grid for station work can replace any one or two sections of practice. Keep in mind that it is easier to run a grid practice when you have a large coaching staff, experienced players, or when using drills that the players are familiar with. Set a time limit for each rotation (4–7 minutes) and encourage players to move quickly between stations. Rotate at the whistle in a clockwise direction and be sure to time accurately. This system is useful for any level of play.

- Form groups of 6–8 players.
- Sub in any of the variety of drills into each individual station.
- Reduce the number of grids if necessary.

In Between	Pair Tag	Score the Try	Bullrush
Fend Off	Partner Tackle	Hit and Roll	Walking Rugby

CHECKPOINTS

- Make practice sessions fun and effective—a little variety goes a long way toward keeping the game exciting for coaches and players.
- Maintain a flexible attitude in terms of planning practice sessions—adjust length of practice and drill focus to meet team and individual needs.
- Practice a play or drill until satisfied with the result—seek satisfaction, not necessarily perfection.
- Encourage constant movement during practice sessions (the more ball contact, the better).
- Remember—good practice equals good game play.
- If you fail to plan for practice, then plan to fail.

GLOSSARY

Advantage — The referee does not whistle for an infringement during play, which is followed by an advantage gained by the non-offending team.

Advantage line — This is an imaginary line that runs through the center of a scrum, ruck, lineout, or maul and is parallel to the goal line.

Back line (backs) — The scrum half, fly half, inside center, outside center, wings, and fullback together make up the back line. Their role is to position themselves to support the forwards.

Blind-side wing — When play is developing to one side of the field, the wing on the opposite (and shorter) side of the field is called the blind-side wing.

Conversion — A placekick or dropkick at goal follows a try. The conversion is taken on a line through where the try was scored (2 points).

Drop goal — A drop goal is scored during play when the ball is dropped from the hands so the ball touches the playing surface and is immediately kicked through the goalpost uprights (3 points).

Forwards — The two props, hooker, locks, flankers, and the number 8 together make up the forwards. They participate in the scrum and lineout.

Grub kick — A grubber kick is made by letting the ball fall from the hands and kicking it along the ground.

Kickoff — The kickoff is used to start the game. The ball is placed on the ground at the halfway line and kicked a minimum of 10 meters forward.

Lineout — The forwards line up at right angles to the touch line and the ball is thrown along the direction of the lineout.

Loose forwards — The loose forwards (the two flankers and the number 8) are the players who are positioned on the side and at the back of the scrum.

Loose head prop — This prop is positioned on the left side of the front row.

Maul — A maul is a loose scrummage in which the ball is held in the hands and clear of the ground. One or more players from each team are in contact around the ball.

Moving in depth — A player is moving in depth when moving along side but slightly behind the passer. This allows the player to move up and take the pass correctly.

Offside — A player is offside if he or she is in front of a ball that is held or kicked by a player on the same team.

Open-side wing — The open-side wing is positioned on the side of the field on which the back line is formed (wide side of the field).

Penalty — When a player has infringed the rules of the game, the referee will award a free kick or a penalty kick to the other team. A penalty kick may be taken at goal, or it may be taken down the field or as a tap penalty.

Penalty try — A penalty try is awarded between the goalposts by the referee against the defending team because of a foul play that, in the referee's discretion, has taken away the attacking team's opportunity to score (5 points).

Ruck — A ruck is a loose scrummage in which the ball is on the ground. One or more players from each team are on their feet in contact over the ball.

Scrum (scrummage) — A scrum is formed when the two teams close up in readiness for the ball to be put on the ground between them. The scrum is a method of restarting play.

Tap penalty — This occurs when the player taking the penalty taps the ball with his foot to restart play.

Tight head prop — This prop is positioned on the right side of the front row.

Touch down — A defender may ground the ball in his own goal area. The play is restarted by a 5-meter scrum from the goal line if a defender carried the ball across his own goal line. A 22-meter drop-out occurs if the attackers put the ball into the in-goal area.

Try — A try occurs when a player first grounds the ball in the opposition goal area (5 points).

ABOUT THE AUTHOR

Brian Quistberg has been involved with rugby as a player and coach for more than 20 years. A graduate of McMaster University (physical education) and Queen's University (education), he was named Rugby's Coach of the Year in 1989 (University of Waterloo). He continues his involvement with the sport, now coaching rugby at the high school level.